A Charge to Change

"Taking Authority Over My Life Situations"

Jermaine Weeden

WESTBOW
PRESS®
A DIVISION OF THOMAS NELSON
& ZONDERVAN

WestBow Press books may be ordered through booksellers or by contacting:

WestBow Press
A Division of Thomas Nelson & Zondervan
1663 Liberty Drive
Bloomington, IN 47403
www.westbowpress.com
1 (866) 928-1240

ISBN: 978-1-9736-1981-9 (sc)
ISBN: 978-1-9736-1982-6 (hc)
ISBN: 978-1-9736-1980-2 (e)

Library of Congress Control Number: 2018901763

Print information available on the last page.

WestBow Press rev. date: 3/23/2018

Contents

Introduction

When I imagined the things that I would accomplish in life or things that I wanted to accomplish, I must say that I never envisioned myself writing a book. I never thought this was something I could do. Writing this book has been a long journey. I went through many days of having writer's block, and I just couldn't concentrate. I realized that some of the blocks that I endured were for a reason because I learned so much more information after those periods of time. When you grow, you experience some great moments as well as some not-so-great moments. Life does have challenges in areas such as finances, happiness, health, relationships, and other important areas. The one constant is learning to go forward while maturing and learning. The one thing I've never done is count my problems or try to figure out how many times something has occurred. I just try to roll with the punches, but I also try to stop them. Life should not always be about bad things and bad thoughts.

My belief is that if you poll a hundred people and ask them about their overall life, whether it is great, average, or not so good, there will be more who say average or not so good. The factor in that type of result should be what we focus on the most. Why would I consider my life as average or even worse? Typically, there are some failures or things that did not go right that prompt an answer like this. I have spoken to many people to determine the pulse of their lives, and so many have difficulties based upon conditions and not being willing to adapt to the changes that occur. When you realize that life often poses a challenge, you have to learn, grow, and educate yourself; every day is a classroom, and there will be homework. Life is figuratively a daily classroom with many lessons given out. There are some daily lessons that we have to come up, but there is always a way to get through it. Some things in life are more difficult to handle than others, but if you really focus, you'll come up with the best possible solution and get through it.

Everything around you changes so abruptly. Some changes are gradual, precise, or even sudden. Changes can be easily solved or can be challenging. Changes can be exciting or exhausting. Whatever you are faced with, you have to deal with it head on. There are many great things to experience in life. Almost everything in life will evolve in some way from its earlier state or condition. Clearly, your body structure will change from a newborn into what you look like at this moment, but the body doesn't stop there. I can do specific things to adjust into my adult years, but it requires me to make some choices in order to keep my body healthy.

In the end, life proves that change will occur, whether you're ready for it or not. If I had to rate my life at this moment, I would tell you that I've had a great one. I'm not just saying that. I really would say it has been a great life. I can't rate it as average or bad just because I've gone through some difficult moments throughout my lifetime. I see it like this: Just because I fell off my bike the first time I got on it doesn't mean that I don't find enjoyment on my bike. I just had to learn from the fall and delay the excitement until after I mastered how to ride. Can I tell you this? I loved riding my bike once I learned, and still to this day, bike riding is a hobby I enjoy. The fall that occurred while learning just taught me that I don't like that feeling, and I needed to work harder to avoid that experience.

Life can be viewed like that; some things we encounter may hurt, but if we get a chance to do over, then so adjustments and focus could lead to us not experiencing some falls and failures. My grandmother once told me that in life, you have to look for the positives because sometimes, the negatives are much louder and bigger. There is an old saying that goes, "Where there's a will, there's a way." I actually believe that if your will is strong, then you can overcome anything. You may not be able to change what has happened, but you can determine how to get through it.

One of the greatest truths I ever heard was that when your ceiling continues to be raised, you still have room to grow. I will say that to anyone who reads this: You still have room to grow. I believe death is the ultimate point in which you stop growing. You will hear this throughout this book: Every day you awaken into a new day, you have to raise up your level of expectations. Your grind has a lot to do with your expectations as well as your hunger to be better and to succeed in life. You should always strive for better. We can look in the mirror and always find an area that we can improve, but it will require some changes, whether in thinking, actions, or effort. My take is this: You should never wake up wondering what will go wrong that day. Instead, counter those thoughts by saying, "I'm going to handle whatever I may face."

This book will give you encouragement, but it will also empower you. At one point or another, we all have moments where we're filled with feelings and emotions. It is actually okay because we're all human, and life issues can take us to some very dark moments. I may have emotional moments, breakdowns, and lapses, but I try to keep myself strong enough to not have a mental collapse. Your mental stability is very important in order to rise up from any and all adversity. You will find that most people struggle when circumstances present a different outcome from what they were expecting. In this life, you won't see everything coming, but you should know you have the ability to make good things happen.

Bodies change, money changes, styles change, people change; therefore, you should be aware that change is going to happen some kind of way. You can face many challenges over a lifetime, but there will be great rewards for meeting the challenges head on. When I began writing this book ten years ago, I found myself having so many distractions, and I went several days and even months without writing. I thought about this one thing that I have heard writers talk about, and that is having a writer's block. I never actually understood what it meant, other than a writer gets stuck sometimes and has nothing to write. I found out that your surroundings have a lot to do with the desire to write as well as deciding what to write. Around this time, I was dealing with a lot of issues personally, professionally, and certainly spiritually.

The next couple of years were some of the most troublesome times I ever faced. I may have been experiencing a writer's block, but life was providing me the content of what to write about. Many days, I found myself sitting in front of my computer, just pondering what to write while all the time distracted by outside issues. I would type a little, but I had a lot to say, even though nothing was coming out. Writer's block is "the condition of being unable to think of what to write or how to proceed with writing." Look at the first part of that definition, which says "unable to think." That got my attention right there. I was dealing with so many changes in my life that I just could not think. The definition explained that it's a psychological thing that inhibits you from writing. *Psychological* definitely stands out, which means that it's mental.

The definition also says that writer's block is usually temporary. So my question was that if it was supposed to be temporary, why did it continue? The answer was me and my surroundings. I just had so much going on that I didn't take the time to put myself in a comfortable, stress-free environment, which would have helped me get more done. I would have definitely finished a lot sooner. I just had to move or deal with the blocks, and as you can see by the book, I did get through them. This book will answer so many questions in your life, but my hope is that you also get other ideas when you're facing a difficult change. I will certainly tell you to get all you can out of this life and enjoy the great things it has to offer. Yes, you may not have had everything happen the way you expected, and you may have fallen down at times, but you also got up. You just have to remember that the power is always in you.

Older people used to tell us when we were kids that "it takes work to get the things worth having ." This says to me that happiness, joy, and peace will take some work because they are definitely worth having in our possession. My hope and prayer for people is that we learn to embrace certain situations mainly because I believe that there is something significant for us to get whether it is more confidence, strength, maturity, or just educated so that if ever faced with certain scenarios again, we have history and now a blueprint of how to handle it and come through much easier than the previous time.

Foreword

By Kevin Whitaker

First, I would like to thank my dear brother Jermaine for allowing me the opportunity to share in this incredible project. I've personally watched this man develop into an incredible leader, one who understands the call and responsibility that God has placed on him. This book has been developing in him for years, and now it's time for it to manifest. There is so much to be said about change. However, I'll make an honest attempt to share my thoughts on this subject; I'm well acquainted with this subject matter due to some changes made in my own personal life. I believe that change is a necessary and in many instances a natural progression of life. In other words, there are some things that change inevitably, such as us getting older, and as we get older, our bodies change, and our children become adults, go out, and get married while possibly becoming parents; henceforth, we become grandparents. These are considered natural progressions of life, but then there are those things that life presents us with that we must take control of, or should I say take charge of, in order to manifest change. I firmly believe that wherever you are in life, if you don't approve of or agree with something, you can change for the better. You must be willing to do what's necessary in order to change, and although change can be challenging, you'll find that it gives you a better perspective on life.

In order to change your life, you must change your mind. And to change your life, you must also change the company you keep. The Bible teaches us that Paul wrote letters to the church in Corinth, Ephesus, and Galatia, and these letters were written in essence to challenge the people to change their minds concerning certain issues. In Romans 12:2, we are charged to change; it reads, "Be not conformed to this world but be transformed by the renewing of your mind" (KJV).

This word *renewing* implies a complete change for the better, which suggests to us that change should be progressively moving toward who and what we desire to be. Now when you talk about changing the company you keep, 1 Corinthians 15:33 says, "Be not deceived: evil communications corrupt good manners" (KJV). This word, *communications,* is better translated as *associations.* Therefore, it matters who I allow in my personal space. We are charged to change.

I want to announce to you that in your effort to change whatever obstacles you may face, the grace to overcome them is also available for you. We must understand that God will not be outdone by the devil and his ways. The Bible says that where sin did abound, grace did much more abound; therefore, God will step in when it appears life is overwhelming and the enemy of life is getting the best of his children. We must also understand that if we belong to God, then he is just as responsible for us as we are to our children. We are charged to change. When you read this book, you will hear Jermaine share practical information that can help anyone who's feeling the charge; he shares from personal life experience and shows how he overcame trials, with the help of God, and is yet overcoming every restriction placed around him. So in this book, you will learn about life and what to do when you're feeling an urge to change. You will learn how to navigate through life's obstacles and do what is necessary to change. I believe this book will help those with low self-esteem to get charged by seeking God and allowing him to awaken the greatness in you. This book will invigorate you to think on a different level and also to accept certain responsibilities for your personal change. Read this book with an open heart. You will be challenged; you will be motivated; most of all you will be charged to change.

Chapter 1

Change

Life sometimes can be exhilarating, exciting, and meaningful, but it can also be tough, difficult, and challenging, and there are many other thoughts that come with a wide variety of emotions. The one constant theme about life is change. Life can take a course all on its own, but you have to be the owner of that change. If you could write the script on change, then you would likely direct it in a way that's easy, effective, and designed to fit your thoughts of how it should turn out. In many cases, you can write the script, but you just have to be aware and be ready for the hidden plots that may pop up during times when your story is being written.

As I think about my life's history, I must smile because of the way things happened and because of the person I have become, the person I was shaped to be. Growing up as a young boy, I was always taught that a man should be tough and strong. For most of my life, I think I lived up to that. It was throughout this process that I had to learn that toughness didn't mean I was void of feeling. I grew up thinking that if you cried or if people saw you cry, you were weak or soft. I've come to understand that crying does not make you weak or less than a man, but it allows you to release the inner emotions that you are feeling. Many people who hold in so much pain, hurt, rejection, and frustrations, which only cause greater emotional damage and even physical harm. I have learned (more often than I would like to admit) that we all have our moments. When people go through life with so much bad history stored in their emotional memory banks, they eventually find themselves having a breaking moment that can negatively impact their lives. I just want to say that we all hurt, but we should all heal. So many people do not know how to heal. Just like the weather, life changes constantly. You can never truly prepare for all changes that you might have to face, but you can learn to overcome them and be successful.

Throughout this book, you will hear me say that change is necessary. I say this because it is true on so many fronts. A word that comes to mind when talking about or going through change is *adapt,* which we will discuss later on in the book. I will say this one point now regarding the word *adapt:* You have to become skilled at adapting in order to become settled in a situational or personal change. There is a well-know saying, "Progress is impossible without change, and those who cannot change their minds cannot change anything." This is a powerful quote, because if we look at the essence of what is said, progress can be stalled, halted, or nonexistent if we don't want to change, especially our thinking. In most cases, struggle may be the requisite, but it will be the meaning of why you had to change. Struggle is just a stepping-stone to progress. You have to change the way you look at things in order to establish how clear of a vision you have to be successful.

As I look over all the changes that I have endured in my life, the first step toward change is being aware, but the step after that is acceptance. It would be much easier to pack it in and quit, but that will only further put you in a negative spiral of having hope and believing in yourself. Many times, people don't see that change is needed until it's too late. Your happiness can be on the line if you don't see what changes are needed in your life. I also see people who refuse to see changes that are needed or required because they have gotten comfortable and come to the thought that change may be a waste of time. Don't delay a blessing because you are unwilling to change an area of your life due to fear.

Let's backtrack a little now and look at the word that is the inspiration of this book.

First, let me state that the meaning of a word provides us with general knowledge of the word but also gives us a glimpse of the impact that word can make. The meaning of a word also gives us a broader view of the impact needed to understand a particular thought, and it shows us the reason why the word is used. When you look in a dictionary, every word in the English language was designed with a significant meaning, but some words have monumentally more significance than others. I really thought I knew what the word *change* meant, but after looking up the definition, I found that it has more precise meanings that will get you excited about change and broaden your understanding. As you go through this book, you'll see how change is essential and necessary. Change is something that you cannot always control, but you can certainly adapt to it and adjust to it and come through it with a positive outcome.

Let's look at the word *change* and its meaning.

> Change: to make different in some particular way; to make radically different; to give a different position, course, or direction to; to make a shift from one to another; to undergo transformation and/or transition; to alter or modify.

We see change every day of our lives. I often look at how the weather can look one way but then can change the next minute. This is a change that none of us can control. Without notice, the change can be beautiful, refreshing, pleasant, uncomfortable, scary, or even troubling, but you have to manage it and adapt to it. The sun may shine or the sky may be full of clouds, but you still have to accept it. The reality of the matter is how well you can adjust. Life may have its challenges and uncertainties, but you still have the chance to make the best out of the situation.

There are always going to be things that come upon you suddenly, but the Bible says that the Lord God is your refuge and very present help when you are in trouble. Change pushes you to levels you've never experienced and can be used to motivate you to do greater and better. You are prompted to examine your situations and evaluate your outcomes. To say you would rather have things stay the way they are seems a little misguided because change is always coming. Most people are okay with what they see when they feel that it doesn't readily affect them. But oh, boy. When it affects you, then it's like the world is truly turned upside down. You can sometimes turn a blind eye to what you really see or a deaf ear to what you really hear, but this often is a negative because it takes you out of reality or delays an action that is needed.

Oftentimes, your thoughts, or the mental pictures you construct in your mind, may not actually be the reality of what is occurring. In your mind, it is easier to not deal with a situation than to deal with the issue and be hurt by it. I must say that peace will only come to a situation when there are answers to all questions or when you have initiated and received closure. Leaving a situation unresolved only leads to a situation worsening or prolonging a needed result. When you choose to avoid a situation or issue, you only allow that situation to determine when it will manifest. And as most things go, it will be at an inopportune time that may cause more pain and suffering than dealing with it sooner and just living with the results.

I will now be the first to tell anyone to trust in God and deal with a situation head on and live with the results. If you do what is right and handle any circumstance with a focused and clear mind, then the result may surprise you and turn out positive. You definitely need to have some faith.

Have you ever had a situation that required change in a particular area, but it was very difficult to even understand how to go about the change? Change can be perceived as good as well as bad. The one thing that most people fear about change is the void of assurance that is involved. Change shifts you out of your comfort zone. You miss out on many things in life if you are afraid of change. If the truth be told, many wonderful business ventures never come to fruition because someone is unwilling to take a chance with change. Most of us have gone through certain things that distorted our thinking and made us wonder how we were going to get through it. Did you ever wonder why change is always said to be necessary, but you generally don't feel that way? When I think about change, it puts me in the mind-set of change of direction. Occasionally in life, you are put in a crossroad situation, where you must decide which direction to take because the old way is no longer working. There is a reason why the old way is not working, but you still try to keep that way life, which keeps you from moving forward.

Oftentimes, God will close off a certain direction that has caused you trouble or pain. He will also choose another direction for you if your old way conflicts with his plan for your life. In Isaiah 43, God said "Behold, I will do a new thing" (KJV). In order for God to do a new thing in your life, he must get you going in the right direction. New should be expected daily. New should be viewed as exciting and joyous, but sometimes, you may see it as daunting or negative. I believe new should be welcomed because it means that it is the replacement for something old. Change will get your attention.

We all have taken certain roads or paths that led to a wreck of some sort. If you had a GPS for your life like you do your vehicle, you would have chosen the right way, with some occasional detours for the construction moments of your life. The goal of a GPS system is to pave out a way that will get you successfully to your destination. Actually, you may not have a physical GPS system, but God is your spiritual GPS who controls the way for you, naturally and spiritually. God has given us his Word to lead us and guide us through any tough situations. Psalm 119 says, "The Word [Bible] is a lamp unto my feet, a light unto my path" (KJV). God has given us the best direction to take, which is a life lived after him, which will lead us to our eternal home: heaven. In the meantime, while trying to make it to heaven, you will face many challenges and go through many changes in life that will test who you are to get to that place of peace, hope, and joy. You have to keep on the path designed for you, or the path you end up on will require rerouting to get where you wanted to go. With the right guide, you won't end up lost if you follow the map put there for you. A map is designed by someone who knows the path, has designed the path, or has walked it themselves.

Chapter 2

Power through It

There may have been times over the course of your life where something happened you were not prepared to handle, which birthed the thought that you didn't have the strength to get through a tough situation or the power to make a hard decision. I am pretty sure that even if you thought you were strong, some situations made you question that strength. When you go through a rough stretch, it can be difficult to find yourself and get it back together. Through every rough stretch and through all the challenges, storms, and trials, you need to maintain and keep your joy. You go through trials and tests and find yourself searching for answers that don't seem to exist. At this point, praying, talking to God, seems strange, as if you've never spoken to him or sought him out before.

Then, when you can't find the answer you need right then, when you're searching for it, you typically go through an emotional roller coaster and find yourself dealing with frustration, doubt, and maybe even panic. After feeling this for a long time, you may develop heaviness or have some confidence issues, which can lead to discouragement and bouts of depression. We all have been put in precarious predicaments that took us for a loop. You suddenly look up, only to come face-to-face with change. It took something difficult to happen in order for you to make some important and key changes to your life.

The fight within a person plays a major part on the decision to bring about change. Mark Twain said, "It's not the size of the dog in the fight, but the size of the fight in the dog." The size of the dog is not always the determining factor for victory when you are in a fight. The fight may be a tough one, but you have to be tougher. Fear is the one thing that you can't take into a fight. Thank God that he fights our battles. Your heart and passion can win out over bigger obstacles, as was the case with David and Goliath. David's fight (heart) on the inside was far bigger than the giant Goliath. David had once fought and killed a lion and bear that were much larger than his natural frame, but the fight in the bear and lion did not compare to the belief and fight that was in David. He felt that he was superior because he believed in God; he believed that nothing was too hard as long as he had God on his side. David remembered the stories of how God brought the children of Israel out of slavery in Egypt through many miracles such as the parting of the Red Sea, destroying Pharaoh's army, and knocking down the walls of Jericho in order for God's people to be witnesses to his power and love.

David faced Goliath with the greatest asset that we could have, which is faith. Most people believe that a stone used in a sling could not kill a nine-foot-tall giant, but history shows that faith can have the same impact as the stone used by David, as well as faith and belief, which can overcome life-altering conditions such as sickness, cancer, car accidents, natural disasters, and much more. We all have some Goliath battles in our life, but we have to believe in God and believe in ourselves. I believe these things are far bigger than Goliath could ever be. The fighter in you plays an important part of dealing with tough issues as well as major choices you must make. The one thing that most people forget is that there is a fight in us all, called our will. There is God's will and our will. Your will in you has to be well. Do you have a well will? You must have a strong will to make it through tough battles. Sometimes, you have to will yourself to get through. You also have to make sure that God's will for you matches your will for yourself. When you think of the will that I just mentioned, it only means having that push and perseverance inside of you. Philippians 4:13 says, "We can do all things through Christ who strengthens us" (KJV). My understanding of this is, we can overcome obstacles because of the faith on the inside of us and because Jesus died for us all to have abundant life and overcome the spiritual tests that we are often faced with. This scripture does not mean you can do something silly or irrational; you can't accomplish anything just because Christ lives in you. Once you believe in your abilities and realize that God has equipped you from the womb, then you can see that you had it in you all the time. The Lord will not put you in any situation that is harmful or tempting, but your choices and decisions can put more on you than you can bear to face. After changing up some areas of your life, you will see how powerful you are when you believe in God; he will then give you insight into what he's called for you to do in your life. Change will require a lot from you and will take a lot out of you. As I said at the beginning and will state throughout this book, change is necessary.

Over the years, I think back to my good days but also to the days that were not so good. It just got to a point where I just realized that I needed to have an open mind so I could focus on the changes necessary in my life so that I could shift the balance of good in my favor. I learned that God's perfect will for your life will interrupt your own individual plans. When you begin to understand God's will and purpose for your life, then you will know how to remain in his will. You can struggle with this if you're not patient enough to allow a natural, needed change to take place. We want what we want, when we want it, where we want it, and how we want it. This is good if it happens the way you pictured it, but what happens when nothing seems to fall in place for what you thought? "Give up" should not be the answer when the chips don't fall where you want. The difficult things in life have a way of making you determined, focused, and decisive about what direction to take. I find that most people, including myself, work better under pressure. I'm not saying you always want to be in a pressure-cooker situation, but those moments stretch your thinking and force you out of your long-term comfort zone.

Many people can't handle the pressure of making difficult decisions. This is why I respect true leaders because they have to deal with so much and still lead the people. When I think about stories of people who have gone into the military, they all detail the experience of basic training. Basic training is what its name suggests: The training is basic until there is live action. The training covers a lot of areas but can only be proven effective when put to the actual test. That is when you learn if your training produced a good soldier. Patience will help your focus, and great ideas will be birthed as you carefully weigh the pros and cons to a situation. By exercising your thinking, you stretch your own mental capacity. I can say that I'm a better thinker when it comes to making decisions that may change my current view. The one time that you will find it a little tougher to gather thoughts is when you are frustrated, angry, or depressed, only because these distractions consume your mind. I believe you can thrive when thinking rationally and going through these four steps of decision-making: planning, evaluating, analyzing, and designing. Most people try to accomplish a task with just a whim or a general thought. Throughout history, famous people had great ideas of what they wanted to create and how they wanted it to look, but it would have never been possible without planning. The Bible says that without a vision, the people perish. Let's look at that scripture for a moment in regards to a great idea or vision. When God instructed Noah to build the ark, he gave specific instructions on how to build it, what to build it with, and where to build it. God showed Noah the details and even described who could be allowed on the ark. God literally gave Moses a blueprint that he carefully designed himself. The vision was successful because God backed it up with planning. The greatest victory to this accomplishment with the ark was that God had to choose the right person to carry it out. Moses was the best choice. You can't have a vision without a plan. It takes focus and planning when dealing with change.

Next, Noah evaluated the reason behind the Ark and what factors that he had to deal with building the Ark. Noah determined that there was no one willing to sacrifice themselves because the people were more concerned with worldly pleasures, not their eternal existence. Noah heard from God that a major change was about to take place; no one else even had a clue what was about to happen on the earth. The word *plan* means to do something in advance; all things are thoughts before they are actually visible in the natural world.

Then, Noah had to analyze, which means he had to examine the factors and decide how to build the ark. The result would be a place to cover him and his family from the storm that was coming, but he also would have obeyed the command of the Lord.

Sometimes, when change is about to happen, you have to key in on the factors but also consider the results. Noah had to clearly decide that he was chosen to carry out God's will and know that even though he had no carpentry experience, that God's blueprint was enough to be successful. Noah examined carefully in detail in order to identify the key factors and complete the vision. The designing stage was instrumental for Noah because of the cargo God said had to be on the ark. He had Noah to gather all types of animals, male and female, some big and some small, tall and short. The ark of course had to be designed to hold all of these types of animals, as well as the eight people, including Noah. If God had just told Noah to go build the ark and not provided any specifics, I'm pretty sure he would have failed, mainly because he was not skilled in that area.

Moses clearly showed his ability to think and handle adverse situations because when he killed a man, he quickly figured up a way on how to stay alive, evade the Egyptians, and avoid punishment. We all can think fast, but are we fast enough to be successful when times are changing? Change is necessary and will require planning, evaluating, analyzing, and designing in order to determine the risk or reward. The word *risk* means to have a chance of loss. When you think about this in regards to change, the potential for risk is what drives people to not want to change. The thought of loss normally controls your attitude toward change. As I look at it, there are risks with most of the things in life, even with the things we do or say every day. There is always the possibility of some level of risk.

I have also seen that with risks come rewards. You already know that change definitely has its challenges. You could also look at financial risks in retrospect; millionaires often say they took major risks in order to gain their success. I try to see risk as an opportunity to think, assess, and implement. There is always a benefit gained from the right type of change. I will dare to say that some of the rewards you will receive will be in areas such as your growth and progress in life, your family, professionally, spiritually, mentally, and physically. The risk that we face with most change is that we can't handle failing, but you have to attempt the change if only to say that you tried and gave it your best shot.

I guarantee that with the right amount of focus and effort, change can be successful. I didn't say "easy" as the obvious word because not everything is simple. Some risks that impact me may not affect others. Yes, there will be naysayers, doubters, blockers, and opponents who will try to hinder your progress, but at the end of the day, you have to be the master of your own fate. People may be the cause for a change, but you need to write the result. When people are a factor in you trying to do something positive, you have to be determined, no matter what. Make up in your mind that you can do what needs to be done.

Chapter 3

Rejection Prompts Change

How many times have you been rejected? Did it put you in a tailspin of emotion? Did you go into the situation feeling already defeated? Did you learn from your rejection? Did you overcome the most hurtful rejections that you experienced? These questions could be thought of in regards to the many different results of being in a bed of rejection. Rejection has caused so many heartaches in my life, but I am thankful that I made it through each one. The most hurtful rejection typically comes from a loved one. Some people you may have helped, the main characters in your life's book, may reject you or turn their backs on you. Being rejected by a stranger is easier to overcome than by someone you know.

It is sad to say this, but most people will remember rejection more than they remember the great accomplishments in their lives. Rejection can leave mental scars if you allow it. I try to be open to other alternatives before I approach a situation. I am the type of person who expects disappointments, but I hope for the best and certainly look for great outcomes. I try to go into a situation with an open mind. I will weigh the option that something could turn out differently than I expect, but I go in with the belief that it could be good. I'm not oblivious to the idea that rejection may be the outcome. In some cases, rejection was so devastating that people committed suicide; that rejection may have stemmed from a loved one, job, opportunity, or idea. You have to approach life-altering moments with a clear and open mind. This strategy prepares you for anything.

In the beginning of this chapter, I asked a series of questions, including how you felt after a rejection. I wanted to talk about that topic because your views after being rejected are key to your future outlook. Many people are just torn up inside when faced with a burden of rejection. They lose confidence as well as hope. Recovery times from rejection are rarely quick, but it must be a short-term recovery. You don't want to lose many days because you will not be able to regain them. "Time is money" is a statement that I have heard many people say over the years, but to me, time is precious. Don't lose a big chunk of your life because of a rejection. I understand there are serious rejections we all face, but we have to find that inner strength and fortitude to move forward.

You also have to replace that rejection with motivation; if you don't, it takes you into another question I asked at the beginning, in regards to feeling already defeated when approaching a situation. Rejection causes deep scars that may cause a serious lack of confidence. Rejection can also cause low self-esteem. This often accompanies rejection. Let's be honest: You are human, and you hurt, and it throws you for a loop; it may take you a moment to gather yourself and get back to who you are in order to regain your mental stability. I can say that some bouts of rejection have caused me to slip into depression. You feel so low and down because of rejection. The feeling of rejection is terrible, and for some people, they may never recover. Some types of rejections that could be destructive involve relationships, jobs, and personal affection. The most hurtful part of rejection is that someone didn't act the way you were expecting. As I think about it, you put so much mental effort into a situation that it devastates you when you're rejected. A relationship rejection hurts because you may have put in a lot of time and effort, emotionally or physically, but it may not have been what the other person wanted. I've seen so many people unable to recover from this type of rejection. I heard it said that there's a blessing in every lesson. I certainly believe that's true. You may not see it right off, but one of the greatest teachers is life. One thing for certain: Life is a classroom filled with many assignments.

In my experience, a big advantage is when you're able to see the rejection and can avoid it. Rejection can push you or punish you. Why let something punish you when you know what you're trying to do and believe it's for the best? You have to build your hope on what you know is important and what you desire to change in order to get to your next level. You can't have doubters and nonbelievers in your corner; they will just talk you out of it. There have been days when I was rejected, but there were also times I've been rewarded after a tough rejection, where key decisions actually panned out. There were some issues that crept up, and I needed to reroute some areas of my life, but I found it refreshing and exhilarating and felt reborn in my mind, body, and spirit after being rejected.

Rejection did that. It can cause some things to be renewed. I have seen rejection cause a major turnaround and improve someone's focus. You sometimes don't give enough attention to ensuring that you're at peace in your mind, body, and spirit. When you're at a place of peace in your life, then the most important thing should be balance of these three areas: your mind, your body, and your spirit. I found it most interesting that I had to be the initiator of such things as new paths, new visions, and new thoughts in order for me to see the good happening in my life. Once I became an initiator, then my next move with creating change was to become an instigator. The word *instigate* means to provoke change. *Instigate* also means to take drastic action. When you see an area of your life that is not moving, then you should feel a push to take drastic action; you are the best judge of what is better for you, your life, and your future because it will affect so many others that could benefit from you doing something greater.

You have to be a great instigator for your success and make some drastic changes in your life. A few years ago, I was diagnosed with a bad heart valve, which could lead to congestive heart failure. The doctor said that it was dilated above the normal size. I then took that as a challenge to get in better shape and fix this on my own. If I knew some physical changes could help my health, then I would just do it. I remember working hard to lose weight; this put me in better health, and the doctor told me a year later that my heart was back to normal. I had to be an initiator and instigator for my condition to change.

I could also be an irritator, which I will explain. Many times, you get discouraged or frustrated because things haven't lined up for you, but you often have to point the finger at yourself. Being an irritator means you can go against new visions, paths, and thoughts as well as causing a delay of your destiny. I can clearly see that it is my time or season, but because of my unbelief and my doubt, my destiny is delayed. In most cases, you know what you should do, but you're reluctant to do it. I don't want to die and miss out on so much more when all I had to do was change.

We are irritators, especially when we fight against the good we deserve and what is destined for us. When I was growing up, I'd hear people say, "The devil is a liar." The fact of the matter is that he is a liar, but you should not lie to yourself when truth is staring you right in the face. I know that I can effect change because of what I've been through, and so can you, if you just desire to do it. I once heard a minister say that we are made for more, and I believe that whole heartedly. The one thing that I would add to that powerful truth is that you have to know your worth, and if something does not add up to that worth, then you must begin the process of change. When you don't know your worth, you can do things that continue to devalue you, whether it's giving your time to the wrong people or venturing into areas that are unproductive. When you are productive, you increase your value. Always know that your value is based upon you and not anyone else's perception or opinion. My dad always told us that if you don't stand for something, then you will fall for anything. Falling for anything can lower your standards, and then you are subject to accepting mediocrity. This is the time to decide that accepting mediocrity is not an option. If you are going to work hard at something, then why not let it be the best?

Chapter 4

Change Is Personal

Most people lack confidence because they don't value themselves or their thoughts. I'm not saying you should become arrogant or so full of yourself that you create a better-than-thou attitude, but you do have to have that necessary swag and confidence about you that makes you feel good about yourself and who you are and the good example you are becoming. So much of who you are is tied strongly to your identity and the general belief of who you are and where you belong. If you don't have an identity, then you are not really envisioning yourself for the better. I realize that so much of a person's identity is nonexistent, but it doesn't have to be that way. It make take awhile before you come into the knowledge of the type of person you are, but you'll get there eventually. Why would you suffocate just because you have yet to find out who you really are in life? Why would you disappear because you have not found out who you are? Why die and exit this world not knowing who you are? You can have a smile on your face all day long and still not know your identity. If you are always being who others want you to be, or if you are who others say you should be, then you are their thoughts instead of your own person.

When I grew up, I was a big kid, and I struggled mightily with my identity because of my lack of confidence. I felt that you had to look a certain way to be part of the crowd. I was often teased because of my size and wanted so badly to change my looks. After a while, I would find myself believing the things being said to me. I didn't realize this at the time, but their thoughts of me formed an identity of someone different from who I really was. I used to cry many days; it seemed like I was always going to be that fat kid, and I thought I would always be judged by what was said about me.

If you aren't strong enough to handle the things people say about you, you may find yourself believing what they said, which could also make you think that the world would be better off if you weren't in it. I took the jokes, but I also thoughts like most kids who are being ridiculed: I doubted myself. I am extremely thankful that I didn't do what so many youth do, which is suicide.

After a while, I just tried to manage it, but it never seemed to work out that way. I remember being relieved when I was no longer the butt of jokes, but I lived on edge, wondering when the jokes would lead back to me. Kids would be checking or playing the dozens, but I often noticed that when someone else was being picked on and everyone was laughing at them, that person would say, "What about Jermaine?" meaning me, just to get the jokes off of them. Things like this will sometime create someone totally different, and you may find yourself reacting to the negativity and question who you are because of others.

For me, I had to realize that I had the power to be who I wanted to be; I didn't have to feed into their ignorance. Your demeanor should be solely created by your personality and not by others. People may see you smile and even notice your joyful spirit, but they don't see how hard it is to maintain that smile. For me, some people had no clue how difficult it was to walk through each day, just keeping my head held up high and loving myself for who I was. Many people today struggle with their physical appearance, mainly due to a lack of confidence. I had friends, but I found myself just blending in so that no one would notice. I was very unhappy as a youth; I faked many smiles, and this became the norm for years. As I look at it now, it is somewhat of an oxymoron to think that I could blend in, being six foot three and about 280 pounds.

Opportunity knocks for us all, and my chance came toward the end of my high school years. I had to believe that I was going to be better in the end, and as I look at things now, I am better because of it. Many people go through life and never recover from traumatic events, whether small or large, but it takes a determined mind-set to not allow negative moments to derail your path in life. Life can be great, but it can also present challenges. I may have peace now in my older years, but it took focus. As I began to focus on the positive things and saw some great changes in myself, it changed my outlook on life. Yes, I eventually came to the conclusion that I had to keep believing that I would break out of the inferior shell and break through to where I was the best me that God created me to be.

As I look back over my younger years, I have so many regrets. I'm not talking about the regrets caused by my lack of confidence, but the regret of not accomplishing some personal goals. I could have done some of the things that I thought passed me by, but because of my mind-set, I will never know. I can't blame others for my feelings, but I fault myself that I allowed people to distort me or my path. It's easy to say what you're going to do or what you won't do, but you don't know until a scenario presents itself. I was the fat kid growing up, but I grew up into a man of faith. Your suffering can become your sermon that turns everything around for you. After my spiritual turnaround, I found out who I was and who I was meant to be. I take every lesson learned and use it as motivation, each and every day. I remember those years, not to dwell on sadness but to reflect on how far I've come in my life. Faith in God includes faith in his timing. There is a time for everything, and right now, my time has arrived again. I say "again" because I once missed it, but I thank God for allowing the clock to reset.

We go through many seasons in life, but the greatest season we will come to is due season. Ecclesiastes 3:1 says, "To everything there is a season, and a time to every purpose" (KJV). When you do what is right in your life, your season must come. It is in that season that you reap the good that was sown. The Bible says that if you don't get weary while doing well, in due season, you shall reap. You have to reap when you didn't give up and quit when life got tough or when circumstances were not in your favor. The word *reap* means to gain or win. When you successfully go through changes and face obstacles, but you made it anyway, then you gain and win because it is your due season.

Ecclesiastes 3:2 also says that change is certainly part of our lives and may occur in each of our seasons: "There is a time to be born, and a time to die, a time to plant, and a time to pluck up" (KJV). One of the greatest moments that a person will experience is the time of birth. Wow. *Birth* means beginning or coming into existence. This is so important; your first day of birth is repeated several times during your life. When you exit the womb, you are experiencing birth. When you graduate school, you are experiencing birth. When you realize your purpose, you are experiencing birth. When you go through times of pain and make it through the many changes as a result of the pain, then you are experiencing birth. When you stop walking in someone's shadow, you are experiencing birth.

Your birth is determined by your first day (beginning) and your coming out of a designed place, which means you are coming into your own existence. Once your identity is established, you go through the birthing process. Let's be real: Some births are not easy; they can be hard, long, premature, or late. When my son, Jataire, was born, he was premature and undeveloped; he came into this world in poor health and nearly died coming out of the womb. The message about birth is that there has to be the right time to be born. Your situations have to be the same way. When you do something out of your season and without focus, the birth can result in something dying. Freedom must live and has to be birthed often. Ecclesiastes 3:2 also says there is a time to plant and a time to pluck up. Planting means establishing, but in order to establish something new, some old things have to be removed (plucked up). You can't start over fresh with old things causing your new to be stalled or hindered. It takes uprooting some old thoughts, people, and ideas out of your mind first, then out of your space (environment), and finally out of your life, if they are not meant to be in your due season.

The key to a new season is not allowing irrelevant ideas to remain rooted or going back to a time of your life that is no longer relevant. I once read this on a sign: "Old keys will not open new doors." The one caveat to this is that when a door of opportunity arises, embrace the chance to experience something interesting and fresh. I believe you can make some things happen for you if you just focus on what you want, but you definitely must have vision. When you have vision, you experience many ideas to go with that vision. Many times, all it takes is an idea mixed with some excitement, and you having an increase of high expectation to spark some new things to open up for you.

Chapter 5

Don't Regress

M any people, including myself, regress when they don't realize that change needs to be focused on every day. You have to give change its proper attention. Change is like a lot of kids today, who are spoiled; like kids want more than the normal amount of attention, so does change, which warrants attention just the same. Having the same mind-set year after year can sometimes suggest a lack of growth and highlights the areas of an individual's regression. In this chapter, the focus is on what you can do to keep evolving as a person who can create success and add memorable accomplishments to your life. We've discussed an array of topics thus far, but I believe that this chapter has the most impact due to the need for truth, which will help propel you into a better position in life. Everyone wants nice things and wants to be recognized as successful. Only a very small percentage of people want to remain average, probably due to not having the necessary confidence or self-esteem to make an impact in their lives.

I want this book to motivate you and encourage you to live the life that you have before you and use the power you have inside of you. There is a phrase that I have heard my whole life, and it has been proven: You have to crawl before you walk. Crawl still suggests progress and movement. Then, after a while, I should be ready to walk, which will then cause me to move at a swifter, steadier, and faster rate in order to get where I want to go. I went from a crawl to a walk, and after mastering this movement, I will learn how to run. "Run" implies hurrying up to get where I want to be. Even with the concept of running, you still have to use wisdom and not be in such a hurry that you fail or return back to where you started; it can be difficult to bear if you put in so much time and effort, only to have to start over. Starting over can still be a positive result. Most people would rather get it right the first time, but it doesn't always happen that way. In all that you do, you still have to have patience because it may take just a little more time than you originally figured.

As you have seen thus far in this book, I am an advocate for knowledge. I love to look at the meaning of a word, especially when I need to gauge a certain outlook or perspective. The word *regress* means a few different things. The first definition I saw for this word was that it means to go backwards. This is interesting because so many times, we think we're doing what's necessary for the right reasons, only to find that we haven't moved forward at all; it seems as though we're just going backwards. Some people are comfortable even though it seems like nothing has gone right in their lives. There's a reason why God didn't give us eyes in the back of our heads. We were made to go forward and, most importantly, see what is ahead and not focus all the time on what is behind us. This is more of a mental and spiritual analogy because physically, you sometimes have to turn around, but in order to have spiritual and mental growth, you can't focus on what's behind you. There was a reason that it was given the position called the past.

The second meaning for the word *regress* that really stood out for me and really formed the topic of this chapter is that the word means "to revert back to an earlier or less advanced state." All I can say right now is, "Wow." This regression occurs in most people's lives, whether in business, personal situations, spiritual advancements, relationships, or emotional. We revert and regress far too much, and then the areas of importance in our lives are readily affected. There are probably more areas, but these are the most obvious ones. There are times when you may have had an idea to make something better and it didn't work out, but you realized the old way was the better way; this was the better solution. This is not what I am about to discuss. I am talking about when change is evident and necessary, but because of prior failures, doubt, fear, or faltered attempts, you'd rather revert and go back because you are just too comfortable with the way it was. You are not willing to push harder to make some necessary changes that will result in positive results, which could mean more happiness, establishment, prosperity, growth, and even a healthier environment. I am guilty myself of reverting, whether it is an old habit, place, or even a relationship. You struggle with so many emotions and feelings that you conclude that going back is your best option. You will diminish your value and think things like, *Maybe that relationship is not as bad as I thought* or *Being mistreated on the job is all in my head*, when actuality, the relationship is probably that bad and you were correct in what you were seeing at work. You may see discord in your family, but you downplay the situation. You are not crazy, but you are actually craving. I mean, you are seeing what is happening, but do you want to change it? You should want something better, but if you do, then you have to crave better. Oftentimes, just because one of your choices resulted in something negative, you'd rather go back and deal with the conditions of discomfort you experienced, but it was those conditions that caused you to look for another alternative. This is typically how you think, in most cases.

I have to point out the part of the definition that emphasized "going back to a less advanced state." I gather from that definition that sometimes, going back puts you in a declined or decreasing state, when your life should be increasing. If you sit and think about things, what is the gain to keep going backward or reverting back to old habits that only caused you discouragement and unhappiness? This typically cements you into a particular place in your life because most of the time, you will find yourself not moving at all, with something holding you back. Enough has to be enough when it involves staying stuck in a rut. Reverting back into a less advanced state, whether in life, body, or mind, is just not where you want to end up.

There are so many resources that are at your disposal, but you just don't use them enough. Some people feel that reverting back is their punishment. Some see it as the only option. Going backwards to a bad or negative place, even if it's mentally, can affect others close to you. In most cases, this is mainly due to the lack of a support system, whether it be peers, family, or friends. It's very hard when you don't have friends in your corner who could help with your growth, but some people are even more determined just because the odds are stacked against them. Who am I to judge anyone who feels that the fight to create positive change is not the right move? It's not always worth the hassle; when I was really struggling, and it seemed like I wasn't going to come out of a situation or there were obstacles in my way, I had to assess the situation. I've heard others use this phrase, as well. Everyone in life has to assess their own personal situation, but I can say that sometimes, the situation doesn't give you a choice as to the outcome. You may have to act upon a situation whether you have support in your corner or not, and if that's the case, it's going to take perseverance, prayers, and belief in yourself.

When I think of regressing, I think of loss and decline. I think of regression as something that keeps me idle or still, even when I want to go forward. All of us need some help from other sources in order to make it. I just want to make sure I do everything possible not to have to revert. I may not always be successful with attempts to grow, but I don't ever want to look back and see a bunch of what-ifs. I don't want to be that person who always wonders if I could have done something but never tried. Who knows? I may have been able to accomplish what I had so much doubt about. The only way to for you to really know is to try. The failure is not because the attempt failed, but the failure comes when you don't at least give it a try at all. You may question what the use is, but there has to be a factor that you focus on that will aid in your motivation. You can't let every stumbling block or obstacle keep you from going forward with your dreams, goals, and purpose.

I will say again that going backwards should not be an option. One thing I've noticed with people is that when you don't have a good support system in your corner, you tend to give up without looking for resources. When you don't have anyone, you have yourself. I believe that when you have Christ in your life, you were made to go forward and live. You don't want to just be here on earth existing, but you should live. Don't get in a place where you are dying and regressing rather than choosing to live.

You may say all this is easier said than done, but I promise you that if I did not endure it myself, I wouldn't even speak on it. Here is something for you to think about: Every day of the week is going to come, whether you're ready for it or not. I know that January is coming, no matter what, as well as the rest of the months. The next second, minute, or hour is coming, and you can't stop it. Even though you can't stop time, you should use that time to better your position, which should be to keep moving ahead. You just have to make up in your mind that you were meant to be change, bring change, embrace change, and control change. Don't lessen your life by going backward because of fear or doubt. For once in your life, change your mind, and you will then change the outcome.

One more comment on regressing: When you regress, you leave room for time to totally set in and become content to stay just where you are. You don't want years to go by with you realizing that you haven't moved an inch. Make the move right now. If you put in the effort, it can be the right time to move ahead, while leaving behind all doubt and disbelief. In everything that you want to accomplish, there has to be a high level of enthusiasm. You have to maintain your enthusiasm, which means to stay eager. Your eagerness is driven by your passion. There are certainly times in your life where you may not feel the passion to push, and sometimes you just want to leave it be, but you deserve the best. You can't let anything take away your passion. Your passion is what drives your will within yourself. I think about the losses and gains that we experience, which can readily affect our lives. These losses and gains are mainly a proponent of the fact that you may be in denial that some area of your life needs changing. You have to have balance with so many things in life, especially when it comes to your thinking process. You can't always think you are right about everything, but sometimes, you just have to balance your thinking and see the other side.

I have found that prayer is a must in my life. I believe the Bible when it states that we must pray. I will say this in regards to prayer: I believe you must get on your knees and go into prayer many times a day, but everything is not just about praying. Some things are not solely based on prayer; it's about making some necessary choices for your life. I believe that you can pray for God to grant you the peace you need in whatever situation you're praying about, but you also need to make a decision about the matter at hand. Refusing to change can sometimes be a direct result of fear, denial, or pride. The key is that you realize you were created for more. You make things so much harder on yourself by not realizing your value and refusing to adapt to new things, places, or people. I often hear others talk about the fear of being alone to the point where they find themselves staying in a situation longer than they should or being with people who are not worth their time. You can spend countless amounts of energy trying to please people, only to find yourself disappointed and exhausted. At this moment, you realize that being with the wrong person or hanging with the wrong crowd was not the necessity you imagined. We have to evaluate often who we allow in our circle because having that one bad apple can spoil the entire bunch.

A period of isolation and loneliness doesn't mean that you are alone, but it could be that you are in a realignment phase. There comes a point when you just have to go realign your priorities. Anything that is important to your life should bring progress to you and your situation. There is a difference between being alone and loneliness. When you choose to be alone, it is as much of a choice as a result. That time of being alone can be refreshing and a period of evaluation. Alone is not to be viewed as a bad thing, but it should be seen as a mind thing. This should be the point where you get your mind together and in order. When the mind is weak, you are weak as well. Then you are more vulnerable and can't reject what needs to be rejected or accept what needs to be accepted.

When alone by choice, take the time to get prepared in that season of being by yourself so that you stay out of that place of loneliness. You can have a spouse, mate, or occupant and still be lonely. Preparation is the key. What good is it to have someone occupying a spot in your life and heart, but you have no idea of who you are? Loneliness is the state of being unhappy caused by depression because you are without a companion.

Someone may leave you, and if you don't have another companion soon, you may experience this feeling of loneliness. You can feel alone as well, but alone can be fixed easily with family, friends, and loved ones. Loneliness is typically a choice that others make, causing you to be lonely. Both can cause discomfort due to resulting from something changing, whether voluntarily or involuntarily. Either way, change is necessary.

I have found that when you gain peace in your spiritual life, the peace that you can only find in Jesus Christ, you will know his presence is what God desires for you to have. Everyone needs a break sometimes, or you will find yourself about to break. If you don't realize that some things must change, then it could very well be that you lose more than you bargained for, such as peace of mind. Peace of mind is better than a piece of a mind. Think about that for a second. I said that peace of mind is better than a piece of a mind. When you are not whole in your mind, you are not getting a total completion to a thought. I have experienced many times when my mind was all over the place, and nothing ever got settled. I found myself always questioning myself as well as my decisions. When your mind is fragile, so are you. You must have a sound mind in order to have peace of mind. It feels great to have a strong mind, but it's more important to be whole in mind. You should want this same soundness (peace) in your body, spirit, space, and life.

The key to change is having a place to insert that key. Trust me when I say this to you: There is definitely a place or an area in your life to put those keys of change. When you find that place to put that key, then just begin the next phase of turning it, turning it around, turning the corner, or turning it over (to God). Let me be honest when I say that turning it over to God and turning it around is not always easy. Turning things over to God will require you to let down your pride and humble yourself with belief that he will work out any situation for you. When you fully turn something over to God, you have to stop worrying about it and start expecting good things to happen. I know this sounds like a cliché because so many people say this, but I have seen it work. I had to do my part, but certainly God did his part because he had already promised that he is our present help in our time of need. Turning anything around is initiated by the strength of your mind before any action takes place.

Chapter 6

Remain Positive

A key component to changing your atmosphere simply means you must believe in the change. I live by this formula today:

Positive Mind-Set + Positive Words + Positive People = Great Days

This is not always an easy thing to maintain, due to the many different dilemmas that one may face during the course of life. I must say that your focus should always be on having great days and going through life with more peace and happiness rather than sadness and sorrow. This formula brings a presence of peace and tranquility daily to my life, no matter the outcomes, tests, failures, or victories. I push myself to allow each day to bring enjoyment in daily pleasures. When you can train your mind, then you will train your outcome. You should also know that when you change your mind, you change your life. The outcomes of certain issues will determine and reveal your level of tolerance. If you made it once, then you have to envision making it again. Thinking positive is not a hoax, but it is a help. A hoax is something that is intended to deceive. Thinking positive will benefit you tremendously by just creating a mental lifestyle of hope. When you train your thoughts with more positivity and hope, you train a defense for the mind, which is the area that gets attacked the most. We battle more mentally than we will ever battle physically. Our spiritual battles are tough as well, but we fight so much with our mind that we lose more often than we win. A free mind leads to a refreshed body. A free mind leads to a healthy body. God made us to be intelligent beings because the Bible says we were made in his image, which means that we are creators. We have a great capacity for knowledge as well as thinking. The mind holds so much of our emotions because of the way we are wired and the way we think.

Thinking positive gives us another option to combat tough circumstances. A positive mind-set needs to be an attitude and not just words. Positive thinking needs to become a lifestyle of who you are, which helps you to be the type of person who looks for better options rather than the ones sometimes given according to the situation. Proverbs 17:22 says, "A cheerful heart is good medicine but a broken spirit saps a person's strength" (NLT). This scripture proves that having a cheerful nature through positive thinking is good for the body, mind, and spirit. When you are cheerful and positive, it gives you a physical boost of health. Your mind can be the root of so much of your stress, which can cause much harm to your body. When you are cheerful, little things don't even matter to you. When you remain positive and cheerful, you then have a need to maintain that good mood and happiness, which will then take precedence over anything trying to ruin your mood.

I used to be bothered when I saw someone who was always cheerful. I realized that it bothered me because I had nothing good going for me at the time. I probably experienced more down moments at a period of time in my life and didn't even try to be cheerful. Doctors say your moods have plenty to do with your health. I have had bouts of depression caused by stress that affected my health through high blood pressure and headaches. One time, I went to the doctor for a checkup, and I had so much on my mind that my blood pressure rose to stroke level. The doctor asked if I was worried about anything, and the answer was certainly yes. In that moment, my thoughts were focused on heavy things, which could have cause a terrible outcome. In order to have faith, you have to have positive thinking as well as positive beliefs. You have to empower your mind as well, so that when anything comes against you, you will not default to negative reactions. Scientists have proven that a positive mind can aid in healing sicknesses such as cancer. This is such a powerful revelation; the mind is so strong that it can play a major part in physical healings. You hear all the time that when people come back from a terrible illness, they state the condition of their mind was critical; they had to maintain a positive mind-set if they were going to recover. Therefore, if you know that your mind is a powerful resource in having peace of mind, then you need to utilize it.

Your mind is a powerful tool that can help you adapt and adjust to any change that presents itself. You just have to think the necessary thoughts you need to remain a help to yourself. Positive thinking and positive words can be contagious, and they will certainly bring a smile to someone who needs a kind word. Speaking positive words to someone who is in need will bless them, as they may be going through a tough period in their lives. I can't count the number of times when people have said thank you for a kind or encouraging word. What they may not know is that I had to get to the point where I stopped thinking negative about everything and transformed my thinking. I dwell on the positives but understand that everything is not always going to be perfect. People tell me all the time that they admire how I approach life, but I say sometimes in the back of mind, *If they only knew.*

I have found that being positive and helping others will often will help yourself. Proverbs 23:7 says, "For as a man thinketh in his heart, so is he" (KJV). This scripture says to me that I can form a reality in what I may think. If I think defeated, then that thought takes over, and my countenance shows defeat. If I focus on something bad, then bad will be the outcome. You may not believe this, but your mind is just that powerful. My thoughts added to my words can frame who I am, whether at that moment or for a specific period of time. If I think I am healed, the Bible says I can be healed. If I think I can overcome, then I will overcome. It all comes back to how you think and what you think; if that's the case, then why not think good thoughts and just choose to believe? Change will test your mind-set; you may have to work overtime to get your thoughts to line up with positive encouragement, but always know that this type of thinking is necessary. Billionaires have documented that they had to remain positive during adversity, which led them to keep pushing, and the reward of that type of thinking paid off.

If you are entering a battle, you can't go with a defeated mind. It would be over before it starts. Go in with a victor's mind-set, and see the results become a benefit. If you are not getting positive people to speak into your life, then focus on speaking positive to others. Give that feeling to someone else's life, and watch how it makes you feel. I don't have time for negative situations or negative people. I have my share of problems that I have to deal with, some tough and some not so tough. Therefore,

Jermaine Weeden

I don't have the time to add a bunch of negativity to that list. I surround myself with the right people who will keep it real with me, but not just tell me what I want to hear. You can tell people the truth even if it hurts, but if you are a good friend, then you can help them through it. Positivity should always be based upon love, compassion, and truth. You know that when you share a certain bond with another individual, you have to keep them motivated, which generally comes from surrounding them with positive energy.

Chapter 7

Empower Yourself for Change

Do you believe in you? Do you believe that you have it in you? Most people will say yes, without any hesitation. The word *empower* means "to be given authority." In most instances, that power has to come from you. You have to be empowered to get yourself through a situation, but you must sometimes empower others, as well. It is a powerful thing when someone is armed with belief. When someone is empowered, their level of potential is great. I have witnessed at particular times when an authority figure would get up to inaugurate or swear someone in; they use the phrase, "I charge you …" followed by defining their assignment, role, or expectation. They would also say, "You are charged" to do this or do that while in stated position.

It totally blows my mind when I hear that phrase; it give the person confidence as they are receiving a new position. I believe that is how you should feel about change because change is a new position that needs confidence, boldness, and empowerment. The only voice that you really want to hear is the one that comes from God because he is always going to be there. God gives you his power daily, but you have to be ready to receive it. There may have been some times when you found the strength to make it but didn't know where that boost came from. In 2 Samuel 22:33, King David said, "God is my strength and power for he makes my way to be perfect" (KJV). I believe this to be true; I know there were many times I was just tapped out because of discouragement, but prayer gave me a boost, and I was able to turn things around because I knew that God loved me. I found strength in just knowing that. I remember all the things

I was taught in church, but mainly that Jesus died on the cross and was resurrected for me, and that gave me the power and hope that I needed.

Let's go back for a moment and deal with a little more detail with the word *charge*. I looked up its definition, and it gave me a clearer understanding of why that particular authority figure would use those words during an initiation. Look at the definition:

> Charge: power given; mandate; to distinguish; to take inventory; decree

Once you understand the meaning, you begin to see that it represents everything strong and powerful, as well as something definite and sure. Motivation and strength are needed to accomplish the job, assignment, or task ahead. To say "I charge you" means to say that you have the mandate and power to successfully complete a task. The importance of this statement is vital when you have to face change. There are not many feelings that can compare when you have that empowerment. You feel that you can accomplish anything. When you are given a charge to do something, you have to receive it and take ownership that something needs to be done. A charge may sometimes be a challenge, but it has to be believed that it can be accomplished. When an authority figure gives a charge to someone, this charge is given with the belief that the assignment has been earned through empowerment and will be done. You should wake up every day knowing that you have the charge to succeed and win. The power within you is driven by a simple thing, a choice. You can choose to dig deep or be dug under. I always believe that you give yourself the best chance when you count on yourself. You should know yourself better than anyone, and whether you believe so or not, there is strength and power in us all. Things may have occurred that caused you to doubt your inner strength, but you have to keep pressing and digging to acknowledge that it is still there.

In 1 Samuel, there is a story involving King David in which he had to empower himself. In chapter 30, David returned from a battle, only to find his camp had been burned down and his wives and children were taken, as well as the wives and children of all of his army. The Bible states that David and all of his men wept so much that they didn't have any strength.

This story shows me that there are so many things that can happen to us that will test our inner strength, but we have to respond with courage and confidence. In this story, after David wept for his family and the families of his men, his trusted soldiers blamed him for what the Philistines had done. The Bible states that David's men were plotting to kill him by stoning him; the bitterness in their hearts grew stronger and stronger.

This was probably one of the most uncomfortable moments of David's life. He not only had to deal with his family being taken, but now his army wanted to kill him because of it. The part of the scripture that really amazed me was that when all of this was occurring, even though David was lonely and vulnerable, he encouraged himself in the Lord. I remember wondering how David encouraged himself while he was about to be stoned, his family was kidnapped, and his home was burned down to the ground, but the Bible said that he encouraged himself. David remembered who he was and the faith he had, and at that very moment, he empowered himself with his belief that he could recover all that was taken from him. David prayed to God for wisdom and received his answer as to what he should do. He stopped weeping, and after he was empowered, he empowered his men, and they went with a determined mind to get back what was taken from them. David and his army defeated the enemy and recovered their wives, their children, and all of their possessions.

I often refer back to this story when I felt like quitting and giving up. I believe everyone at some point in their lives has been down in their faith, and it may seem like no one can help, but I've learned that you have to pick yourself up, encourage yourself, dig deep within yourself, and defeat that problem with faith and determination. It may take some adjusting because all situations are different, but the one steady in any situation that you go through should be the power inside of you. We all like to taste victory, but it may take you to put a little more into it to get that joyful feeling.

One more significant point that I can make on this story is David's position as a leader. He had to lead by his deeds as well as by his words. The situation got as bad as it could get, but he still managed to collect himself and empower his men to believe in him again in order to regain everything taken from them. Confidence is the most significant thing that is planted within the psyche so that those being empowered will feel that they are approved. Confidence is an important factor on the outcome of any situation. Someone once said, "Confidence doesn't always come when you have all the answers, but it comes when you are ready to face all the questions and challenges."

You must always have self-confidence. Life is not always easy, but you must have confidence, which will give you the perseverance you need to make it all the way through. You must believe that you are gifted for something and that this gift will get things attained. Fear can stifle your thinking and shut down your confidence. Fear can put doubt in your thoughts and heart, but this will only keep you from getting things done. Fear will rob you of knowing what the outcome will be (or could be, if you lack the necessary confidence). In many cases, I have seen people struggle to build up their confidence due to failed attempts at change. Confidence will give you that boost to keep trying and develop that "no quit" mentality. It may seem easier to quit, but when you actually look at things, it takes more energy to give up than to see it to the end. The sense of accomplishment when you complete a task will make you want to experience that success all over again.

I went through some crucial times when I had to encourage and empower myself, especially dealing with the condition of my son, Jataire. As I stated earlier in this book, he was born into this world as a premature baby, which led to many problems with him physically. He was born almost two months early. At birth, his lungs were undeveloped, and the doctors did not believe he would make it. He spent his first couple of weeks at the Children's Hospital in Little Rock, Arkansas. They had to give him CPR immediately out of the womb, but thanks to God, he made it. As Jataire grew up, countless doctors said that he would always have breathing issues, and he developed asthma. He's taken breathing treatments for years. There were times when he almost died because his lungs did not develop at birth. I can remember my mom sitting up with him for hours well into the night because he would get sick and have trouble breathing. I was a young father who had custody of my son and my daughter, Aaliyah. I would not have made it through fatherhood without my mom, my dad, and my grandmother. While I worked, my grandmother cared for him during the day until my mom got off work.

Up until about age five, Jataire went through so many days of sickness. He went to the doctor about two or three times a week. The winter months were probably his worst due to the cold weather. He wasn't able to go outside like most young kids because of the many changes of climate. I remember feeling so discouraged because I could not help him. I cried many days while feeling useless and helpless seeing my son so sick, and I couldn't do anything about it. This was probably the most challenging change that I ever went through. What I went through as a kid could not compare to seeing my son this way.

My mom and dad always told me that God was going to heal Jataire, but I had to have faith. At the time, I wasn't really going to church, and if I did, it was only to appease my parents. I was an adult, but you know how subtle parents can be when they want to fuss at you about something you are not doing. I grew up in church but strayed away as I became older. I would pray daily and often for my son, but God didn't seem to be listening to me. I can honestly say that I really didn't have a strong relationship with him, but something happened and I realized that it was time to get one with God. I remember one particular night that I went out and returned home really late, about 2 or 3 a.m. As I entered my parents' house, I saw my mom and dad up with my son, giving him medicine and treatments because he was really sick. My dad said we had to take him to the emergency room because of his breathing. I remember seeing Jataire's stomach extending out as far as it could go just because he was just trying to breathe. I was stoic and didn't know what to do. The first thing I could think of was going to my room to pray. I went to the bedroom, cut out the lights, and closed the door to pray. I got on my knees to pray, and all of a sudden, I heard a voice say to me, "Now you need me."

I immediately got up and turned the lights on to see if anyone was in the room with me. The voice sounded like my dad's, but he wasn't in the room. I shrugged it off and thought it was in my head. I cut the lights back out and got back on my knees to pray. I asked God to take the sickness off my son and put it on me because I could handle it better. As I kept praying and asking God to heal my son, I heard the voice again say to me, "Now you need me."

I freaked out and jumped up to turn on lights, but still no one was in there with me. I then knew that I was hearing from the Holy Spirit. I was actually afraid to get back on my knees to pray because of what had just happened. I opened my door to go back up front where Jataire was, but I stopped because I heard my mom praying the same prayer for God to remove the sickness off her grandson and put it on her. I was astonished that we prayed the same prayer. I stood and listened as my mom talked to God, but I realized that her conversation with him was more genuine and real than my prayer. As she finished, I acted as though we were coming out of the rooms at the same time. In a matter of moments, as we walked back to the living room, we saw Jataire jumping up and down, playing as if he had not even been sick. I saw how immediately God healed my son because of the prayers of his grandmother.

All of a sudden, my mom began to feel bad, and I knew that God honored her request to remove it off of him and onto her. This moment began my desire to get a closer relationship with God. When Jataire was about six, I remember taking him to the doctor, and I was just so down because I wanted my son to get better. I will never forget that day because that was the day I decided I needed to stop feeling sorry for myself and start having some faith. As Jataire laid on the table, sleeping while awaiting some test results, the doctor came back in and told me he needed more meds and treatments. I asked the doctor something that I had never asked before, which was if my son would ever get better and outgrow this asthma. He told me that he didn't think Jataire would ever outgrow it, adding that he believed he would never lead a normal life. The doctor said he would never be able to play outdoors or participate in sports because of his asthma. He basically painted a picture that my son would be equivalent to a cripple.

When the doctor left, I had a moment with God, and then I heard a voice say, "He cursed him, but I am going to heal him." Over the next two years, Jataire began to overcome many of his conditions; he was sick much less than he ever had been. Children know when they are different, and my son knew that, which meant that I had to instill confidence in him. When he was seven, I decided to let Jataire play flag football. This was truly a faith walk, because of me knowing all that my son had gone through and how running and being outdoors could affect him, especially in the fall, when the weather is so inconsistent. He wanted to play, and I was willing to try it. I consulted with my mom, and we decided to give it a chance. Jataire had no clue as to what he was doing, but he was just glad to be out there running around. I was probably the happiest person in the world and didn't care at the time if he pulled a flag at all. He made it through the season without any harm and actually got better in the process. I could not believe that after everything the doctor said, my son was not the same little sick boy. He had moments at times, but far less than previous years.

He did so good that I even allowed him to play T-ball. He did not get sick at all from the air, the dust, or the running. I can truly say that one of the most difficult moments in my life got much better when I started to adjust and just have faith. I could tell that Jataire's attitude had changed, and now he had sports in his heart. When you go through changes that are traumatic or life altering, you need to have motivation and a story of victory. It is a great feeling to taste victory, and you want that feeling even more. Too many times, people play the victim when they should relish in being the victor, whether a physical victory or emotional victory. As a former little league football coach, I know what it feels like to have the smallest amount of chance to win, but the best opportunity to shock the world. Many times, my team was the underdog, with no one giving us a chance to win. It seemed as though we always had the inexperienced, slow, and less talented players on the team. The one thing that I can say that every team did have was players with heart and willing to work hard. I had undersized kids who had a will to play but just needed motivation and teaching. For the next six years, my teams might not have been the most talented, but they were the most unified. I can remember getting kids who had never played the game at all, but I believed in giving everyone a chance, even if we lost.

I found out that if you coach kids up and give them confidence, you'll see a dramatic change in their behavior and in their play. The key to empowering people is encouraging them that effort can sometimes overcome talent. The main reason I started coaching was because Jataire was now playing and wanted to learn. The luxury that I had with my teams was that I had a son who was extremely fast, even though new to sports. Yes, the same kid who had been sick most of his young life, but his previous coach really spent time with him, and he learned quickly. I knew that I would have to empower him and motivate him, as well as the other kids. Being that I was once a kid who had confidence issues growing up, I was the perfect one to encourage these same types of kids. Each year, we would start out slow because of the tremendous learning curve, but we would always finish strong. I believe to this day that you win with a team-first attitude and live with the consequences. I taught my son as well as all of the other young men to look out for your teammate, no matter what. I taught my offensive players that when they scored, the whole team scored. I would preach that the least one made that touchdown happen. I would schedule functions with the team so that they could interact with each other and also let them be kids and have some fun. I talked to them about being just as motivated at school as they were in football. I even used school and their conduct as a mean to warrant playing time, and I had parents tell me to make them run laps because of bad conduct or poor grades. I figured that everyone was not going to be a ballplayer.

The teams that I had were not the most glamorous, but they were the most close-knit group in the league, which led to a great team. We would always finish the season with a winning record but were never expected to win much. There was not a time going into the playoffs where any of my teams were considered the favorites to win. I loved this position and thrived in it because when you are not considered a favorite, the pressure is not on you. The underdog has nothing to lose. I loved motivating the kids into believing that they could win. I would always tell them that teamwork would win every time, no matter the outcome. I preached to them that if they gave the effort, I would put them in a position to win. The greatest joy I had was getting the kids to believe in themselves and their teammates. I taught them that everyone had one job, and if all eleven players did their one job, they would be successful. The results proved this.

Over the next six years, my teams won the championship, and I have the trophies to prove it. We played in games where we were down multiple scores with two minutes or less, or we were outmatched and undersized, but we still managed to win it all with a group of young kids who grew in confidence and had the will to do it for their teammates. The joy I get today from those years is that I saw a lot of these kids grow into young men, and they always come to me to relive those moments in their lives when someone believed in them. To this day, I am still Coach

Jermaine. Through all the changes that I have gone through in my life, I was able to empower them to believe in themselves. You can never let change dictate all the rules and conditions. You most certainly can't let it dictate your inner strength or the belief that you should have in yourself. Sports, jobs, school, and other aspects of life reveal that many victories happen when you overcome obstacles in spite of being the underdog. That means that you have some future victories coming, even if you are the underdog. All you have to remember is that you are the right person to empower your thinking and your faith. The power in you is real; you just have to tap into it. The power in you is a deep well that just needs to be brought to the surface. Pull that power out of you and use it accordingly.

Chapter 8

Change the Routine

One day, the Holy Spirit spoke to me about change and said that people are either on a routine or on a route. When you are on a routine, you are not going forward, but you keep coming back to the same place you've always been. How many times have you wondered why the same thing continues to keep happening? How many days have you wanted things to change but didn't know where to start? The key to beginning a new phase is calling an end to the old one. At times, the problem lies with us being content and not prepared for change because we are comfortable and used to things being a certain way. To sum it all up, this is due to our life being nothing more than a routine.

The word *routine* has multiple meanings. One meaning is a constantly repeated action or usual course of action. Most people have their routine down to the most calculated detail. When you are reliant on certain repeated actions, time can become an adversary, especially if something interrupts you. I can assure you that frustration is always lurking due to the fact that you are expecting that every detailed action is calculated. After a while, you get predictable, with no room for change. Routine also means habitual or a continual habit. How much of what we do is because of habit? We do many things out of habit, and we often don't evaluate the impact of what we say or do out of habit. When you are a person of routine, it is easy to pinpoint your every step. Therefore, think about this: The devil is easily given the direction to take with you because you do the same thing all the time the same way. Change it up a little, and you will see that there are always options available for you. Routine also means something that is dull or uninteresting. When you are in a routine, you can get bored with the issues of life as well as your surroundings; you may also feel unfulfilled. I have felt many times that I needed more, but I kept looking at less. This was largely caused by me; there was no one else to blame.

The biggest area that is affected when you live routinely is when you are in relationships. Don't get me wrong; we all have a system of how we do things, but you need to always keep yourself open for change. You want to have some flexibility and spontaneity. After a while, the one you are with may want something different; people typically get in a place where they won't do things different because they've always done it that way. Routine living is like being in a rut that seems impossible to come out of. Some people feel they are stuck at a place in their lives, but the contributing factor to this is that they are not raising their level of expectation. You have to believe and begin to make things happen. You can't always wait on others to be the source of your survival, but we certainly know that God is our power source (although we don't always utilize him). You will never have that sense of security and belief if you don't stand up and stop the same things from always happening. Routine causes lack in your life, and the result of lack is fear and failure, when God has not created you to be a failure.

I found it interesting that routine also means "usual course of action." This is so true for many people. When you are doing the usual things all the time, the devil is always able to pick you apart. I have seen people stay in bad situations, bad relationships, and other bad environments because they resigned to the fact that things were not going to get any better, nor did they believe the situation could change. Someone once said, "Routines must have a purpose and provide an outcome that we can see and take some comfort from, or else they have no use at all." Usual course of action to me is that you have developed a stagnant mind-set. *Stagnant* means something that is not flowing, sluggish, inactive, or not going forward. The definitions of routine and stagnant have some similarities; they can hinder your growth and development.

There is a story in John 5, where there was a man who had been sick for thirty-eight years. That is a long time to be sick, but his issue was that he was stuck in a routine of waiting, when there was healing for him all the time. He never changed his course of action, which could have gotten him delivered from his sickness much sooner. The Bible says that he waited for the angel to come down and trouble the water in the healing pool, but he didn't have anyone to pick him and put him in the pool to be healed. In life, we can't always wait for someone to pick us up because we may just be wasting valuable time. The Bible says that Jesus saw him and immediately knew that he had been there in that same place for a long time. There is always evidence when something has gone on for a long time or been in a certain environment for quite some time. The question that Jesus asked him was, "Are you ready to be made whole?" (KJV). In order to get out of that routine, you have to decide in your heart and get ready for a change. Instead of the man with an infirmity stating yes to Jesus to his question about being made whole, he began giving reasons why he been in that rut for so long.

Jesus was not concerned about how long he had been there, but he was concerned that the thirty-eight-year-old routine was not benefiting his condition. When you have been in a routine for so long, you begin to believe in your own excuses instead of making change happen. Jesus commanded the man to get up out of his state, pick up his confidence, and go forward. The Bible says that his condition changed immediately, and he found his identity. If the devil has his way with your life, you will live a residually routine life.

The Holy Spirit also said that some people are on a route. When you are on a route, you have direction. It is amazing how the meaning of a word can change your life and perspective. *Route* means a way, a fixed route, an itinerary for travel, and to see something through to completion. As I look at the meaning of this word, *routine*, I get excited; I stopped the cycle of routines a long time ago, and now I see a way. The Bible says Jesus is the way, the truth, and the life. This Jesus is a route. The next definition says that *route* means a fixed route. Jesus died on the cross for all humankind, which means a route. The next meaning says itinerary for travel. I have learned that the Bible is my itinerary for my travel. The Bible helps me to travel my route through this life: the ups and down, good and bad, joy and pain, as well as the journey that we are traveling using my itinerary. That is a route. I believe the most important meaning of the word *route* is to see something through to completion.

Wow. I have to say that again. Wow. How many times have you not completed a mission, task, or something you promised to get done? You didn't set your course of life on a route. Someone once told me, "It's always too early to quit." Our state of mind determines our completion. When you are motivated and determined, you can get things done, but what happens when you aren't in that focused mind-set and let some important life-changing moments go undone? As I think about a route, I think how airplanes, boats, trains, and all transportation operations must draw out routes to ensure that they make it to their destinations. A route is also based upon time as well as distance. A missing route may mean that you collide with something that is also on a route. I have traveled to many states and outside the country, but I never would have made it to those places without a way, an itinerary, a fixed route, as well as the love, passion, and drive of an individual (pilot) to see something through to completion. I truly thank you, Jesus, for giving your people a route.

Chapter 9

It Is You Who Makes Change Happen

In life, we use words like *luck* and *coincidence*, but that says that Jesus is not always capable. Because this book has a lot of biblical truths and references, I want to stay there for a moment. What is luck? Do you base your circumstances or results on how much luck you have, whether it's good or bad luck? The word *luck* is not a heavenly term, nor does that word exist in the heaven realm. The word *luck* means "a series of events that happen beyond your control that seems subject to chance." That statement right there already proves that this word is not from God. Luck is something that occurs when we try to handle something that is beyond our control, which is then a coin flip as to the results. There is an expression that people use that says, "If it wasn't for bad luck, I wouldn't have any luck at all." We create a world of discouragement all on our own, without anyone else's help. Yes, there are some things that bring despair and discomfort, but it still comes back to you making some things work for you in order to turn around a situation. Just as easy as someone can believe in bad luck, why not believe in good luck?

I have never believed in the word *coincidence*, either. Believe it or not, coincidence is tied to luck. They are actually one and the same in regards to meaning. Both words mean something that happens by chance. The word *coincidence* suggests that God does things by chance, and that is not biblical truth. Jesus is our route and not my luck or my coincidence. People often say that everything happens for a reason. I truly believe that is true because we validate the results. I can determine that most of the outcomes we are faced with happen because of our choices, decisions, the people we deal with, or even the places we go. As much as you believe in luck, you should know that God is a sure thing; you can't win with the roll of the dice or spin of a wheel, but you can have it assuredly with a choice. I don't believe in forcing my love for Jesus Christ on anyone. I definitely will not force my thoughts of Jesus on anyone I come in contact with. I believe you have to want him for yourself and allow the choice to be a personal choice to receive and submit unto Christ.

When I am approached and asked how I made it through my rough times, I feel that I have just been invited in, and I most certainly share my story, which involves my spiritual beliefs as well as acknowledging Jesus Christ. I just know that it was my belief in Jesus Christ that provided me with more peace than I could ever imagine. I know there are many alternatives in regards to religion, but I don't concern myself with the others. I chose Jesus as my Lord and Savior, and I will not accept anything else. I believe what I believe, point-blank, period. Am I the best? Certainly not, but I am working hard every day to align up with Jesus Christ, who I believe in. I try hard every day to walk right and treat people with the love that is expected as a believer of Christ. I don't tell people with words that I am a Christian, but I prove it through actions. I'm not the one to judge what others believe or who they believe, but I will always stand firm on my personal belief and will never debate with anyone who believes in another religion. I believe Jesus Christ gave us all the freedom to choose, and I will not change from his approach.

My job as a pastor is not to control your thinking but rather give you an additional option to choose from and allow you to make the choice. God has been the one constant fixture in my life, as I've dealt with many changes. God requires change in many areas of your life in order for your life to be a shadow of his image. The charge to change is important in many aspects of your life so that your walk, talk, and life transformation will align with the will of God. Whenever God has given you a charge to change, difficult decisions and difficult situations may evolve in order for you to go through a total makeover. Change sometimes requires loss of old friends, habits, thoughts, mind-sets, and environments. Change can certainly transition you into a place of advancement. God changes will establish you for positional breakthrough. Change is not easy, but it is necessary. God requires a daily change, which is a constant crucifixion of your flesh. To not change means that you don't think there's anything about you that needs changing. Trust me when I say that I believe there is something about you that you could change.

Change must take place if a situation causes you grief, turmoil, or pain. Change can alter your outlook in so many ways. Typically, you look at the negatives of change and see it as a difficult decision to make, but in reality, when you are in a rough spot in your life, change could be viewed as a positive move because there is only one way to go when you are down on the bottom, and that is up. Sometimes, when things are spiraling out of control, you just have to make up in your mind to change the spiraling and make something good happen for you. It may be just to relax and do you.

In order to change some negatives, you have to implement some positives, starting with strength, which I am sure is on the inside of you. There are three things that most people will experience in their lifetime. I call them the three breaks, which are breakdowns, breakups, and breakthroughs. The topic of discussion is probably about changes, and it is because of changes that many people experience the breakdown. There may have been something traumatic, tough, or damaging that could have caused a breakdown, but it doesn't mean that you literally lost your mind; maybe you just lost some of your will(power). You may have endured through a period of your life where there were some breakdowns in your focus, your mind, your life, your goals, and other areas, but you still had it in you to keep pressing through the tough moments. We all experience mental breakdowns at times throughout our journey called life. You may not have been admitted to a hospital, but you may have felt that you needed to check in to one. Life at times is challenging and hard, but you have to know that God has made you a victorious being, and you have been destined to make it through. Therefore, you may go through a breakdown period, but you will most certainly be restored through faith and belief that you have much more to accomplish and give to this life. You will live an extraordinary life because you are a fighter, and it is your purpose to be great on the earth.

The word *breakdown* can also be looked at from a grammatical perspective: *break* means to dissolve or interrupt regularity. I see it as this that if I am having a breakdown it is because something had to be dissolved or interrupted. We can always hope for the best, but we clearly know that it is not always that easy. Another meaning for break is to overcome. Just as easy as it is to focus on the negative, it takes the same amount of energy to focus on something positive. Therefore, I can see the breakdown as something dissolved or something I can overcome. I choose to be one who overcomes. The one thing that I can't do is allow something to break me.

The meaning of the word *down* means to be in a calmer state. I also found that the word *break* means to be on the bottom. Now, think about the two words together and their individual meaning. I can overcome (break) from being on the bottom (down); this is a much better phrase than focusing on what state of mind I am in causing depression, anxiety, or discouragement. So when you look at the word *breakdown*, change your outlook of the word and let it change your outlook.

The other break that we experience at one time or another is breakups. I look back at some breakups that I have gone through, whether in a relationship with a woman, job breakup, and even a spiritual breakup. The one thing they all had in common was a separation period. I had to go through a breakup to realize that I had some growing to do. I have a saying that I am not struggling, but I am growing. I believe we go through things for us to mature as well as get closer to God. I can't tell you what path you must take, but I am grateful that Jesus saved my life. When breakups happen in your life, you feel that a void has been left, but I have since looked again and realized that it was an opportunity for something more solid and secure to fill what looked like a void (empty place). I can truly say that what may have ended only started something better in my life. Something good may have ended, but I realize that the particular person, place, or thing had to leave in order for something greater to come. I won't say that it wasn't the way I expected, nor was it what I wanted, but for whatever reason, it resulted in a breakup, which matured my life on great levels. It is through some of those outcomes that you learn to humble yourself and get in order things like pride, ego, and selfishness. You don't realize those things are an issue until you go through a humbling situation. I have had many nights of crying and questioning God for some of the outcomes, but I was the conductor and controller of my own fate and feelings. Our emotions at times will cause breakdowns and breakups, but when you get your emotions in order, then life will return to order (or order will begin). I heard a song a couple years back that says "I Desire More" by an artist named Crystal Aikin. When I heard that song, I immediately said, "That's it."

I began to tell God that I desired more, and then I began to experience the third break, which is breakthrough. I have received many breakthroughs in my life over the last couple of years that have totally designed my future. I am walking in favor in areas of health, finances, spirituality, and personal life, and I'm awaiting breakthroughs to hit a couple of other areas. If I had a breakthrough in all areas at one time, then I probably wouldn't pray as much. God knows how to get our attention, and I have made up my mind and heart that he has blessed me with mercy and grace, and I will continue to embrace change.

As you probably know by now, I am a word person and love to work the dictionary. The word *breakthrough* means removing an obstacle, restriction, or obstruction. This is really good because these few words have distinct meanings. An obstruction is something in your way. An obstacle is something is hindering or interfering with you. A restriction is a limitation. This is so powerful that it blows my mind how when change is necessary, there is always something (the enemy) trying to stop us from progress. I've been in bad moments in my life where it seemed as though something was blocking me, interfering with me, and limiting me, but God showed up in a mighty way in my life, and things had to be removed, destroyed, and the limitations had to release me.

If you look at your life, I believe you will find that there were some people or things standing in your way; therefore, those things were standing in the way of your breakthrough. You have to desire to get beyond those obstructions, obstacles, and limitations. 1 John 5:4 says, "Whatsoever is born of God overcomes the world, and this is the victory that overcomes the world, even our faith" (KJV). Change is an opportunity for you, and there is nothing that can stop your dreams, your visions, your future, and it is in you to overcome the obstructions, obstacles, and limitations to receive your breakthroughs. Your latter shall be greater than your beginning. The one thing that is evident is that some things are going to happen, and you won't be able to do anything about it. There are some forces that you just can't control. There are many things that are coming that you can't stop. I realize that tomorrow is coming, whether you're ready or not. You better know that next week, next month, next year are coming, ready or not. The one thing that I now focus on is trying to prepare for the time that is coming, whether I have to prepare mentally, financially, spiritually, or economically. If I know that something is going to happen, then I know there is something I can do to set the scene for what I expect.

The point I am trying to make is that only some things are in our control, and this must be our focus. Let the things that we can't control be before who can control them, which is God. Some people may read this book and say they just don't believe that God can do all of those things, and that is okay. My desire is that this book will open up the strength and power within you and allow you to see that you have more to give and accomplish. You have to own your own convictions, but the key to that is to own them, no matter what. You may struggle if things happen that you're not prepared for, but when you know your life and your path, you can be prepared for anything. You know that people are going to leave; it's something you really can't prepare for, but you can take the time to appreciate the people in your life. You always need to look toward the things you expect in the future, which should prompt you to deal with some issues.

I have learned to raise up my level of faith, which gets me through some tough moments. I have also learned to raise up my level of expectations. When I say that I'm raising my level of expectations, I'm not referring to God because his promises to us are sure and definite. I'm speaking in regards to my level of expectation when it comes to my life. I had to look at where I wanted my life to be and not focus on everything in the past because this can get you sidetracked and off-course. I expect to be successful. I expect to be healthy. I expect to go through life with peace. I don't say this without understanding that there are some things I must put in place in order for this to happen. I am now focusing on the resources that I have at my disposal and using them in the areas of my life that need a little touching up. We all can stand to do a little touch-up in our lives.

God often leads you into change. Change can be extremely tough when it's called for in an area that you've been part of for a long time.

You must choose to take a chance, or your life will never change. A good place to start taking a chance is taking a chance on God. Truly taking a chance on God really suggests that you are willing to trust him. He is first and foremost the one good chance to take. The next important person who deserves a chance to be taken on is you. You should be willing to take a chance on you. Who better to take a chance on than yourself? You shouldn't be so quick to count yourself out because in most cases, you have never counted yourself in. Most often, the one thing that holds people back from taking the necessary step is fear. Fear is devastating when allowed into your mind, body, and spirit. The greatest fear that is evident with many people is the fear of failure. This fear shuts people's hope down quickly. Another common fear that I see often is the fear of rejection. The reality is that at some point in all of our lives, whether in the past or in our future, we are going to fail at something or be rejected. We still have to pick ourselves up and keep trying.

The biggest failure is not trying. When you overcome and conquer fears that you have at one point or another, then you will be more willing to bet on yourself. In some occurrences, you are the only person you can count on. The feeling of accomplishment is a feeling like no other. You should want to challenge yourself to do something you didn't think you could because it will be more gratifying to know that you did it. You can't always allow fear to run your life, nor can you allow fear to ruin your life. Fear is capable of doing both. You have to take chances sometimes in this life, if you want to succeed. I believe that taking a chance is what faith is all about, but it is geared toward taking a chance on God. Fear will grip you so tight that you will not make the necessary steps in order to get through some difficult moments. Fear is one thing that will hold your confidence hostage. Fear will control your peace and suppress even your happiness. Fear is a vision killer and a dream destroyer. Fear is certainly a mind killer. Fear will evict every good thing and hope from your mind. I read an acronym for FEAR: False Reality Appearing Real. I thought this to be very on point and interesting. The interesting thing about this is that fear is just that: false reality. I have said for so long that fear is mental and not really reality. If fear is held onto, it can then become reality, but it's still mentally based.

I wouldn't dare say that fear is easy to overcome, but it has to be in order for your advancement. Fear connects itself to doubt. Faith is the weapon to use against fear. Fear has no place where faith is present. Instead of having fear, you should be fearless. When you are fearless, good things are bound to happen. There are things that God will want for you, but you can't let fear of change stop you. Change ordained by God will provide a sense of accomplishment and victory when you know that it took strength, prayer, and belief in yourself. Sometimes, when going through a change ordered by God, you feel a sense of loneliness and despair, but this is only because God is trying to show you that you must trust in him. Oftentimes, when God has given a charge to change, there is some fear, but God says that he has not given us the spirit of fear. The fear manifests in thoughts of whether or not it can be done, if you can make it through the change, or fear of losing or letting go of a habit, person, or place. Change requires the letting go of something and the picking up of something new.

What good would come from changing? This is a common question that many ask themselves, but you must seek God and look for answers beyond what you see. The answer to "What good will come from changing?" will be determined once you make the bold move to change and gain the confidence from making the decision to change. One important factor when going through change is that you must believe. The charge to change is required for all of us in some area of our life and aligns us with the will of God and positions us for abundant living. Plenty of good can come from a change occurring. A change of scenery can be good. A better job can be a good thing. I'm not ignorant of the fact that some change can probably be a negative, but you have to have a good plan with any change. Change is best felt when you view it as a positive step and not a negative conclusion. If you are a visionary, then you have to look at the past, present, and future of where your vision is going to end up. You have to evaluate and assess your position in order to have a successful vision. You have to make provision for your vision; otherwise, the vision may die. When a positive ending is the result, you will have then answered why you needed to change.

Chapter 10

Why Change?

Why should you change? The answer to that question is sometimes out of your control. Change can be a thought first based upon an occurrence. Change can also be initiated by a choice, a circumstance, or even a feeling. Change is often thought of in your mind, but many times, it never happens. The important thing about change is that it needs a plan put in place for it to be completed successfully. Ultimately, change should be faced with a positive outlook, even if you're in a negative situation. Just saying you want to change or that something in particular needs to change will not necessarily get it done. It takes a strong will, which only comes from within. Your inner strength is so important to being able to make change happen.

There are a few things that prompt us to think about change, why we change, or the need to change. We change for various reasons such as financial prosperity and growth, personal growth, relationships (beginning or ending), environment, habits, faith, family, or health. In other instances, we may be forced to change. Change is vital when you have expectations and goals. For reasons as stated above, change can affect your prosperity by opportunities that may arise in the form of promotion, new job, business idea, or some type of venture that will readily affect your personal prosperity. Many people are afraid to take a job or make an investment, because of fear that it may not work out. Actually, you have a 50/50 chance, but you have 100 percent if you count on yourself. Why apply or work hard to be looked at, if you don't accept the opportunity? I believe God opens doors because of his love for us, our faith, and his desire for us to be blessed and to trust in him, but you also have to believe in yourself.

Also, being unwilling to change can affect your prosperity. For example, you may have personal issues, physical restraints, or even a mental approach that keeps you from receiving financial growth; it can even cause a loss of financial stability. Another example of why we change is because of maturity or personal growth. You sometimes realize that certain things that have always been a part of your DNA or just a certain mind-set as far back since the time of your youth seems to prompt you to just wake up and change your thinking. Other reasons as relationships, God, family, and health can be categorized as always in need of change because of these things. A new relationship will cause some things to change. A bad relationship prompts change. Your health requires some important changes. Your faith demands change. When building a relationship with God, change will be a necessity. As you go through this list, you see there are reasons why you should change.

One thing that I am learning is that time requires change. We go from morning to night, and how you start your day is typically not how you finish it. Your start can determine how the end of your day finishes. Starting out bad is not always the formula for how your day will end. I just believe that if you start out your day in a positive manner, then you have a great chance of finishing that way. You get too distracted by bad beginnings, but need to focus on a great ending. You should establish some daily rituals to help you to make it through each day and learn how to adapt to things throughout your day so you can finish strong. There are just some days that you don't want to get out of bed. We all go through this and have these moments, but this just prolongs getting things going or looking with dread at what you have to do that day. That just causes even more challenges to your day.

I recommend reading a daily devotional to get you in the right mind-set. I guarantee that a daily devotional or prayer will keep your mind reminded when moments of despair arise during the day. I find that music can help get your day going in the right direction. I generally like listening to music that motivates me, strengthens me, and focuses me. I love all types of music, such as jazz, country, R&B, and gospel/Christian music. When going through some mental and spiritual battles, you will find me listening to spiritual music in order to get the encouragement I need. If we tell the truth about it, yes, we all need encouraging. I hated reading books when growing up, but I have found there are so many books written about almost every situation we face. Yes, I often read the Bible, but there are other resources to add to the Bible; however, never read those books to replace it.

You have to open your mind to doing things different if you want to get a different result. The things you do leisurely can be a great asset when change is upon you. I play video games to relax my mind. I say again that your mind has to be strong when dealing with change. My favorite mind-clearing activity is going fishing. When your mind is relaxed, it will focus better. When you are relaxed, you think far more clearly than with a cluttered or distracted mind. Life is full of pressures, but you have to take time for yourself and detox the mind in order to be at your best. My advice to you is take a vacation as often as possible; getting away is the best medicine. It can keep you off other medicine. You don't have to travel thousands of miles, but just get away. You may not be able to afford a trip far away; you can go to the next town or even a venue where you live. You'll see that a change in environment makes a world of difference. I have rented a hotel in the same town where I live, and it seemed as though I was in a faraway place. I just needed a break in the normal environment. The one caveat to this is that you have to go with a purpose to clear your mind and relax; you will need this freedom when change is needed.

At the beginning of the chapter, I asked why you should change. The answer that beats all other answers is that you are changing for the better. I have to say that better is picky about who takes its name. We all want better, and if you don't, then you are living in mediocrity. How can you work as hard as you do, put in the time whether pursuing a career or education, only to stay in the same place? You will find yourself seeing your life as being bored. I love to think of new ideas and ways to doing something that I love or even things that I just have to do. Believe it not, you are innovative, but you just have to expand your thinking. You also have to expand your capacity to think. The key to this is not just stopping with the first and easiest answer you were able to come up with. You should always have multiple options, and then you can choose the best one available. Some of your ideas may not be viable, but at least you considered that idea as an alternative. Another thought for why you should change is to show growth within yourself. You may have started out in kindergarten, but through perseverance and hard work, you graduate. Think about this: Some people got stuck and kept having to repeat a grade, but they decided to quit because they were embarrassed. They didn't look at the big picture that if they just keep at it, they can put their lives in a much better position than always having to accept less just because they quit. You should never quit; you lose the satisfaction of experiencing growth, which is the result of adapting to change. Sometimes, it just takes working harder to make changing easier.

Chapter 11

Change Is Daily

It's inevitable: You will face different situations every day. Some types of change occur daily. Change is constant, and you have to deal with it in real time. Sometimes, you may not see clearly the reason for change, but you may feel it. You will often question yourself many times and even wrestle with a decision that needs to be made in regards to change, but at the end of the day, you need to carefully consider the pending benefits as well as counting up the pros and cons. I embrace change now because I learned that there are benefits to positive change, and I like receiving the rewards of change. You face so much stuff in your life, and it can be overwhelming. I can't count the many times I just wanted to give in and give up. There are things that happen that you just get tired of fighting. Your head seems to be spinning from all the reoccurring issues. You make one step, only to be pushed back five. There are times it seems as though you're right there, but you then realize you're not even close. "No pain, no gain" is an expression that people use when hard work is required to achieve greatness and success. Personally, I'd rather have the gain without all the pain, but that's not always the way it works. The meaning behind this reasoning is that it takes strenuous effort, whether it's physical or mental, in order to bring you gain. The notion is that the tougher it gets and the more you endure, the greater the reward that comes from this level of effort and work.

I can say that I do believe in hard work, and I can testify that hard work does pay off. The thing with that is, you have to push yourself beyond what you normally do or beyond the point that you normally reach. You have to be practical about this pain. You don't ever want to push yourself so hard that there is no gain. You shouldn't push yourself to a point where you break. You want to be able to push yourself enough to where you see your growth. The hard work added to the accomplishment of what you are striving to achieve should have a great effect on your confidence and self-esteem. When you are able to see the end, and it's a positive end, you want to be able to say you did it. What person doesn't want to see the fruits of their hard work? You should want to be able to reflect back on the journey, which will show you just exactly what you have accomplished with hard work and effort. This type of mind-set will get you motivated to do even better and work even harder.

I've been working since I was eleven years old, and it was hard work at the beginning. I had no choice but to work hard if I wanted to keep the job. I used to work in the field, where it was hot every day. The one thing that hard work teaches is that you learn to appreciate what it takes to be successful. You learn discipline, time management, and other strategies that follow as you move on to other jobs and careers. It's always good to work hard and give your best effort because someone is going to notice you; this is why so many people are giving promotions or put into even better situations. I watch a lot of sports, and you can see whenever someone was faced with changed and it required more work and more effort because of it. How hard you're willing to work will definitely show up in the work that you produce. I don't understand why someone would not want their best work to be what viewed by others.

When change approaches that requires you to step out of your comfort zone, approach it head on with a good work ethic; don't let the work get the best of you, but turn the table and get the best out of it. I read a quote from Lou Holtz that says, "Winners embrace hard work." He is a championship-winning coach and led many successful players, and I believe he has a right to this saying. I can only imagine that it took a foundation of discipline, teaching, coaching, and belief in the players that they could achieve success. This accolade will last throughout the history of Notre Dame.

As you watch sports and hear the stories of the players, they always speak about the long hours they put in to be good at their craft. I know it seems like we have left the meaning of this chapter, but we are still in the essence of the topic because when you deal with change, it takes perseverance along with hard work. Put the time in, and then you will see the results.

Margaret Thatcher once said, "I don't know of anyone who has made it to the top without hard work which is the recipe, though the hard work will not always get you to the top, but it should get you pretty near it." I'd rather reach the top after giving my all to something than exert little effort and go nowhere. If self-gratification is a reward you receive from hard work, then you should walk with your head held high, just knowing you were able to reach a milestone through giving it your all.

During a time in my life when I was really going through some things, I opened up my Bible and happened to stumble upon a chapter that helped me change my mind-set about the changes I was going through. In the first chapter of James, I received some powerful instructions that help mold my positive thinking. In chapter 1 in James, the second verse reads, "My brethren, count it all joy whenever you face trials of many kinds" (KJV). Wow; this was what I needed. As I pondered what this scripture meant, it puzzled me at first as to how I could be joyful when I was in the fight of my life. I further thought that there was no way to be joyful when dealing with difficult moments and abrupt changes to my life. I reflected back to these discouraging moments, I must admit that most of the things I endured or overcame made me stronger. I learned that whenever you come through a situation, you gain more wisdom. It took awhile, but there were some great lessons learned from every trial I faced.

When I looked over the scripture again, I began to think about how you must hold your head up when you face tough and difficult moments in your life. I came through some rough patches in my life, but what can I tell someone who is not a believer about faith? How can you have faith when facing challenges that are driving change in your life? How can you have faith if you've lost all hope? These are just some questions that I thought on. Not everyone will believe what I believe, but there has to be something they can hear that will awaken them on the inside and help them get through tough moments. The one thing I can say about the scripture verse about counting it all as joy is that anytime you go through something hard, it's an opportunity to gain some awareness about who you are and what can you do to make it through some trial. Yes, I believe that a relationship with Jesus Christ is the key for me, but as an individual, you have to believe for yourself whether he is the way for you. I do know that it starts with you. You just have to know you.

Then the next scripture reads, "Know this that the trying/testing of your faith will give you patience" (KJV). I felt something happen inside of me when I read this second verse. That's not all. The next verse, verse 4, says, "Let patience continue to develop for when patience matures, you will be perfect and entire not wanting anything" (KJV). I must pause for the cause right there. Now, I looked at these two verses to determine where I was with my faith and with my patience. I realized some key things as I reflected back on my life. The trials that I faced taught me patience; some things came up that I was not able to control. The one significant thing about this is that time is your biggest challenge at this point. You worry about things you can't control. Oftentimes, you are so impatient, you tend to add more stress and worry upon yourself. These scriptures say that if you have patience, you will eventually see what comes from this situation. The scriptures are mainly trying to teach you that you have to trust God and let him complete the work that he intends so it will work in your favor. We all need to see things happening for our good and not feel that everything we touch fails before our eyes. God wants to see his people flourish and prosper. We are the ones who want what we want, when we want it, which often leads to it not manifesting. Seeking something you want before it's ready can then be considered a waste of time because you will have exhausted a lot of time and effort, only to have it incomplete.

I immediately realized that I needed to be patient and watch how things developed. Oftentimes, you don't have patience when change is needed. How many times have you rushed something due to your impatience? The result is that the situation did not turn out the way you wanted. You must give something time to develop or work itself out; this is something that many people miss due to not having patience. The word *patience* means to be quiet. It also means perseverance and diligence. If you have patience, you have composure and stability. This definition has just described a blueprint for success. I now understand the scriptures that say you can certainly count on God, but you have to be patient and persevere. Trials that you face may be the very thing you need to unleash the fight in you. Patience is not always a simple thing to have, but it is a necessary characteristic to possess. So many things require patience, but you need to be at the top of the list as an individual. Building anything worthwhile requires time and patience.

The Bible teaches me that patience has a process, and it must go through the process for it to prove its benefit. The process should accomplish three important factors: The first factor about the process we go through is that it must produce our maturity. Everything happens for a reason, but what will you gain from it? Maturity should be your gain when you face changes that are necessary. Another factor about going through the process is that you should be more focused on your goal. In order to get progress from the process, you must learn why and focus on where. Learn why you are going through the process, but turn your focus onto where you are trying to get to. The third thing that the process should reveal is validation. Every step, every loss, every failure, and every gain should validate where you are and where you're going. The fact that you complete the process will validate the faith you had in yourself.

As I recall what I read in the Bible, I remember how Jesus was patient, even when his time of death was approaching. Moses had to be patient in order to see the salvation of the Lord produce for the people. There are so many other examples, but the one common factor was that there was a great benefit to having patience. Take this nugget with you from this day forward: Your patience will eventually pay off, but let patience get you to the end so you receive the payout. There are more nuggets that I found in the first chapter of James. One scripture stuck out to me and fitted me to a tee: James 1:8 says, "A double-minded man [person] is unstable in all of his ways" (KJV).

I believe this scripture fits a lot of people. We are so undecided about things that we never really know what we're capable of because of indecision. Being double-minded means you are always wavering. How much success can come to you if you're always undecided? When you waver, you're really in doubt about what you want to do, say, or think. When you waver on an issue, this proves you have doubt. If you don't trust yourself, then who do you trust? You can't go through life always wavering on your decisions and choices; this type of thinking only prolongs an issue. A decision has to be made. Before I make a decision in my life, I try to weigh all of the options and also weigh the cost of my action. After I have done this, I can make a conscious decision on what is best, based upon the options that I considered. When you are double-minded, you probably struggle with confidence issues. Hebrews 10:35 tells you to hold on to your confidence, which will be richly rewarded. There are great things in store for you when you maintain your confidence. I have said it throughout this book that change is necessary. You just have to believe in yourself and remain confident.

Chapter 12

The Power that Is In You

I have found that prayer helps in so many situations. Prayer is not about quantity of the length of time, but it is about quality of the prayer and the genuineness of the request, which results from the intimate relationship you have with God (or the relationship you desire with him). If you feel you don't have that relationship with God, you can develop one. Psalm 86:5 says, "For you, Lord, are good, and ready to forgive; and have plenty of mercy unto all of them who call upon him" (KJV). In order to begin an intimate relationship with the Lord, confess or repent, and then call upon him. Most people will tell you that so much more is required, but once you give God your heart and mind, the process immediately begins. The Lord longs to speak with you. Change is far more possible when you allow God to lead you through unfamiliar places in your life. I meet many people who exhaust time, money, and other resources and still never grasp the joy and peace that comes with life. I can't see myself always being in a mental, spiritual, financial, or physical rut in my life. I was once there but never felt good being in that place. Therefore, I had to make some decisions and do something about it. Some choices were voluntary, which means that I initiated them, and some were involuntary, and some things may have forced my hand. Life has more to offer me than being stuck in a place when that time has truly passed.

I wake up most days with the thought that it's my time right now, and I shall live and not die. I will run and not get tired or weary. I am the head and not the tail. I believe that I can overcome any obstacle because Jesus died for us all, and this gives me the right to believe. Being a pastor and mentor to many people, I often witness that many people don't know their potential. I often ask certain questions like, "Why do you doubt yourself?" "Do you not know your potential?" or "Why don't you believe in your potential?" These are important questions to ask when I see the struggle with change that affect people so heavily. There are negatives and positives with the word *potential*. *Potential* means "possible or capable of being or becoming." When you think about the meaning of *potential*, you have a chance for being successful. The word *potential* also means that you are capable of all you can become. This means that if you have potential, you have the ability to handle the task, challenge, or opportunity. The negative to the word *potential* is that you can have all this ability but never use it to benefit your life.

Many people have potential, but they may not have the desire, drive, motivation, or passion to go beyond the mark and make things happen. Why? Sometimes, it's could very well be you. You may just have the wrong people in your corner as your support group. Most successful people will tell you that it takes that special, unique quality to move beyond just having potential. The world is full of many millionaires, but there are many should-be millionaires who will never get to that level because they lack that drive to succeed. I fully intend to prosper the right way because of my belief in myself and what I believe I am called to do, as well as what I am called to change. One day, I was watching *The Shark Tank*, where people pitch their ideas and inventions to a panel of millionaires and billionaires, hoping to get financial backing. On some of the good ideas or inventions, the panel would invest and be given a big nice percentage. I saw some people sell their ideas for far less than what they were worth. The problem is not with the millionaire and billionaires, but the people didn't realize the potential of what they created. Change was staring them in the face because of a thought or invention, which could have brought great financial change to their lives. They chose the quicker way instead of securing something for their future.

There is a story of a hungry man who stopped at a lake where he saw a man fishing. The hungry man noticed that the fisherman caught many fishes that day. He then asked the fisherman for something to eat. The fisherman thought about it and said yes, but he asked the man if he wanted to eat one time or eat for a lifetime. The fisherman stated that he could give him a fish, which would feed him for a day, or he could teach him how to fish and feed him for a lifetime. The idea the fisherman had would take the hungry man out of a place of hunger and give him a trade that could earn him some benefits.

This awesome story teaches us that we should look for the long-term solution and not just settle for what is quick. I looked at the word *potential* and saw another word within that word. The word I saw was *potent*. The root word for *potential* is *potent,* which is a powerful word. I have seen the word *potential* many times, but never saw that word. I looked up the word *potent* and got excited because this was what it takes to embrace change and challenges. The word *potent* is a characteristic and a mind-set as well as an environment. When you believe in your abilities and gifts, you are dangerous. There will be nothing that you feel that you can't accomplish when you are driven with that little something extra that comes from within. The word *potent* means "to be powerful." It also means "to be strong, possessing great strength."

When you think of this word and what it means, it denotes the fact there is some inner strength in order for you to be potent. I often share with peers, congregation, and friends that you have to believe in what is destined for you to accomplish. To think about someone who is potent, it means they will make it. I say to you, don't just have potential, but be potent. 1 John 4:4 says that "greater is he that is in you, than he that is in the world" (KJV). "Greater in you" means that you are past potential, but you are now potent. You possess a power that comes from within yourself. Christians, whether new believers, backsliders, or even sinners, have a power inside that comes from God; and if greater is not in you, there is opportunity for greater to live in you.

Jesus said in John 10:10 that he "came to die for us that we will have life and have life more abundantly" (KJV). It was meant for God's people to be blessed. John 10:10 also says that "the thief's [Satan's] purpose is to steal, kill, and destroy" (KJV). The devil fights against your change, when it is a positive, beneficial, or godly change. The devil hates for you to succeed and then give the glory to Jesus Christ. The scripture speaks about the enemy's motive, which is to kill, steal, and destroy. First, he wants to kill your hope that any good will come to your life through change. He surrounds you with the wrong people or creates such a negative environment around you that you have no hope. Second, he wants to steal any and all opportunities of doors opening and blessings for you that lead to any growth in your life. He knows that if you begin to gain a relationship with God that you will begin to see the traps and tricks that he tries to set up against you; he wants to discourage the vision that God gives you. Finally, the enemy wants to destroy you and your hope. The devil wants to put to an end to your progress. Satan wants to end the changes before they start.

It's going to take determination to not let the devil determine your outcome. Make your destiny happen through the power that works within you. The devil will stop you, destroy your hope, kill the vision, and steal your opportunity if you do not pray and seek God. Stay focused on you assignment, and be passionate about your purpose. I once read a quote that said, "Failure doesn't come from falling, but from not getting up." I believe this is one of the best quotes on encouragement. The quote says that you don't fail for trying, but you fail for not trying. Change is hard, difficult, scary, uncertain, and tough at times, but it can restructure your life and revolutionize your situation.

Chapter 13

Your Reasoning for Change

The reason why you should change is determined by each individual. Your reason for the change is not just because you want it, but because you desire it. Change must be motivated by God in an area of your life where you need help, courage, or confidence. Most people reject change because fear drives the thought of *Why should I change?* You often receive advice from friends or loved ones, but the process of change must be thought out before it can be carried out. You can't change your circumstances without possessing boldness and confidence. Boldness is not always prevalent by speech but rather a determined action. Sometimes, you must be bold in your decisions as well as your steps toward progress. Confidence is required when boldness is ready to be put into action. God made me to be an overcomer, and I choose to believe that I can claim victory in all of my life struggles and challenges.

God has not given you the spirit of fear or doubt. Through the power of belief and trusting in God, you can conquer any circumstance. In order for you to count solely on God and possess change, you must have a relationship with him. He equips me to stand against the enemy and receive victory in my daily battles. When I trust God, then I can trust change. Throughout various experiences in your life, you become accustomed to accepting things as they are and are content with how people treat you. The result of this will find you dealing with periods of depression, uncomfortable moments of rejection, and repeat disappointments.

The one obvious but undetected spirit that is present when God gives you a charge to change is the spirit of deception. The spirit of deception will use your particular situation against you to keep you trapped and bound. There are more people in emotional prison than there are in a real prison. Many people look like they are free, but a certain problem, person, or environment has them in emotional handcuffs. When you are in an emotional prison, it becomes difficult to see the light when you are accustomed to darkness. The enemy wants you to live in fear, turmoil, confusion, pain, and sorrow, in thee darkness, but God is our light and our salvation; who else shall we fear? The Word of God states that nothing shall separate us from his love. The problem is that we look for other people to love us, but the truth of the matter is that until they love God and themselves, they won't know how to love you.

Some people need another person to validate them. Once you know yourself and what you possess, validation will come from yourself. In order for you to love someone, you must love yourself. This is why we are required to change so that we learn the importance of the charge that is given to us. God has given us a charge to trust him in spite of what happens in our life. When God directs you while ordering your steps, he will guide you to a place of prosperity and into an area of blessings. I believe now and forever that God is my way, my truth, and my light. Proverbs 3 states, "Trust in the Lord with all your heart and lean not to your own understanding and in all your ways, acknowledge GOD and he will make your paths straight" (KJV). God is saying that he will lead you into change, and he will sustain you during change and bring you through it. You have to first learn how to trust; otherwise, you will have a difficult time because in some way, you need help or assistance from people.

Sometimes, the battle is not with a person, but rather a thought. Some people who are troubled, confused, angry, or lost tend to see things that are not real. When you lean to your own understanding, you need a foundation of your thinking and rationale. When you are not the type of person who receives advice well, you will generally come up with your own way, which could totally cause you to fall into a negative situation. When you go through change, it is wise to seek wisdom from someone who has been there. Wisdom is important in all situations. Don't for one minute think that you are void of wisdom. You just have to use sound judgment and careful planning, and you will have just exercised wisdom.

Deuteronomy 8 states that God led us into the wilderness to humble us and test us to know what was in our heart, whether we would obey him and the charge that he gave us. Change can be a great test to see if you are willing to succeed. Some changes that you face can be critical to your own personal growth. Change must be planned, implemented, and carried out. At no point should you make a hasty decision that is not ordered by God, but God will accelerate the situation when there has been a mandate for change. The time for necessary change weighs heavily on your mind because there are so many thoughts and feelings associated with changing the situation. Change can sometimes feel like weight due to the amount of pressure that change creates when put into action. The type of people you have in your life can affect how you change (or even if you change). When you put your focus into negative people or places, it becomes more difficult to see a positive reaction. Often, the hesitation with a decision about change is caused by your struggle within yourself, wondering if you can handle it by yourself. For me, I used to look at the ending of a situation before it even began. We sometimes look at what we will lose or who we will lose and develop an anxiety about even trying to change.

If you're dealing with a situation that involves another person, and you believe that a decision may cause you to lose that person, that decision may not happen because people are scared to be lonely. Loneliness can be an important factor that hinders change. This feeling of loneliness is caused by insecurity, but there must be some perseverance so that this feeling of insecurity does not determine your outcome. In order to reach an area where there is prosperity and growth, some things have to be let go; there has to be a period of time where you spend with God. People are so afraid of change because it often leaves them feeling helpless and lonely. If the person, environment, or situation does not add anything to your life, it is time to subtract it from your life.

Trust is a word that has been lost or even destroyed in most people. The one area in most people's lives that needs work is trust. I often ask people who they trust. I ask this question because so many people struggle with trust. Oftentimes, people have been hurt, rejected, or wounded so badly that they lose their hope and trust in others, mainly because they were not expecting the damage to come from a particular person. At some point, everyone has placed their trust in someone, just to end up being rejected, disappointed, mistreated, or abused. The bad part about this is that most often the person who destroyed our trust ruined something in us that runs deep within our inner being. We have heard the word *trust*, seen the word *trust*, but we have a hard time believing in the word *trust*.

I remember seeing an exercise where two acquaintances were chosen to play a game of trust. The instructions were for one to stand behind the other, while the one in front closed their eyes and fell back, with the one behind them catching them so they did not fall. Some people didn't think that the person behind them was strong enough to catch them; they couldn't trust them. What stood out to me with this concern was, what if you don't have the right people behind you who keep you from falling? The thought is that they should at least be able to help you, maybe not physically, but emotionally and spiritually. If I don't believe that you can catch me, then maybe I trusted the wrong person. Of course, a person of about a hundred pounds probably can't catch a person of three hundred pounds, but my point is that you need to have the right people in your corner. You need someone in your life who will tell you the truth as well as have compassion for you when needed. You need someone to be a rational voice and hold you accountable to things that you may have to face from day to day. Can you stand upright and fall back and trust that whoever you have faith in will catch you if you fall?

We have all witnessed the word *trust* in action. It's not always easy to place it in another person. Whether it is a friend, family member, acquaintance, many people lack confidence that will never allow us to believe in them. The word *trust* means to have an assured reliance on one's character, strength, or ability. Sometimes, you can't trust others because you lack self-reliance. You must trust yourself before you can trust someone else. The question you must ask is, "Can I trust me?" The reason for having confidence in yourself directly relates to decisions that you make. Another meaning for the word *trust* is to have confidence or to believe in. You have to have confidence and believe in yourself, which means that change ordained by God will not occur without confidence and belief in yourself. It takes confidence to make an important decision about change. Most fear of changing comes from the earlier subject of lack of confidence and lack of trust. If I can't trust God to help me with my situation, then I can't trust myself to come through the situation. The Bible states that if I seek first the Kingdom of God and his righteousness, all things shall be added unto me. God knows what you need, when you need it, and how badly you need it.

The Bible talks a great deal about having faith, but in order to have trust, you have to plant and establish the seed of faith. When a seed is planted into good ground, it will produce a harvest. If I use my faith, which at first may be the size of a mustard seed, it has the potential to grow into a huge tree. The Bible says that you should walk by faith and not by sight. When going through tough changes, you often look at the problem instead of your faith looking at the problem. When you look at the problem, your faith turns its head, but when my faith looks at the problem, my face watches for the outcome to be victory. It is difficult when you have given something as intimate as your trust, only to have someone disrespect and mishandle it. Most often in our lives, it is the people we love who are responsible for our inability to trust.

I want to introduce a word that was given and inspired by the Spirit of God in a moment of consecration about change and the charge we have to change.

We have become crippled by so many people or things that we have contracted what I call trust deficiency syndrome, or TDS. With this syndrome, you develop a blockage in your heart, and where your confidence and faith are contaminated by hurt, failures, and disappointment. TDS destroys your hope and extracts power from within yourself. When something contaminates your ability to trust, you are damaged emotionally. This is an illness that takes a combative spirit against failure. This type of mental illness shuts down your faith and belief in everything in life and causes you to doubt everyone. It is a bad place to be when you can't trust anyone in your life. TDS can bring about many bouts of depression and discouragement. It will cause you to go through life thinking it's everyone else's fault, when the actual fault may lie within you, if you choose not to deal with the issue. Of course, there were times when people mistreated you, but what hurt the most was that it was people you loved; you didn't expect them to commit a hurtful act against you.

This type of issue can go on for years because the pain and memories are too difficult for most people to dredge up; they just allow that pain to lie dormant for years not, realizing how it can affect their relationships, faith, family, and health. Whenever you try to trust again, you often revert back to this illness because you may see signs of what someone has dealt with; it makes that individual shut down even more, and TDS surfaces again. TDS is just like having an open wound that you don't clean, but all of a sudden, dirt has set in now, causing an infection and making it even worse. TDS has to be dealt with in order for you to develop your love and trust again. Why go through life unhappy and never experiencing the great things it has to offer because of a decision to get over a past incident that caused you to develop trust deficiency syndrome? TDS is curable. I repeat: TDS is curable. Like all illnesses, you have to take your medicine. I mean, whatever happened has happened, but you can't let this be it for your life. What happened hurt like hell, but you can live, love, and trust again. TDS should not have a stranglehold on you.

The syndrome's worst side effects are anger and bitterness. You are now so bitter that it's going to take a lot of work, as well as prayer, for you to get over it. TDS can make you so angry and frustrated that nothing anyone can do or say would remotely matter to you until you're ready to let it go. That anger and bitterness together produce terror in your mind as well as your body. Honestly, no one wants to be around someone who is always angry and bitter. You may not have deserved what happen to you, but you can't blame people who had nothing to do with it. This is a common theme with people who have been wounded. There is a saying that "hurt people hurt people." Whenever someone is hurt, whether it's you, me, or someone else, they often hurt those around them, who actually care for them, causing them to walk away. When this occurs, who does the fault lie with? Holding this type of emotions in you can harm you in so many ways. You have to let TDS go in order for you, yes, you, to go forward.

Think about how many people have an undetected sickness. The only time they become aware of an illness is when it abruptly comes upon them, or they see signs that something is wrong. The bad thing about your body is that you can't always see your mental condition. If you have major trust issues that keep you rattled and doubtful of everyone, it is probably a safe bet that you have trust deficiency syndrome. When you put your trust in the wrong person, the outcome is usually not a good one.

I believe that outside of Jesus Christ, you shouldn't just put your trust in anyone. Trust has to be earned as well as proven. In the past, I have most definitely put my faith in someone I thought I could trust. As it turned out, they turned on me and stabbed me in the back.

Most people with trust issues have been betrayed. Acts of betrayal make you lose trust. Betrayal has various meanings, but they all involve a person's trust. Betrayal means a violation of confidence as well as an act of disloyalty. The one definition that states what most people see as betrayal is disappointed in someone's hopes or expectations. If you were betrayed by someone you trusted, this brought great disappointment because you had high expectations of that person. You regarded him or her as a loved one, friend, or confidant. To avoid betrayal, you have to only put trust in people you have a long-lasting relationship with. If you are putting your trust in someone, you should know personal details about them. When you are betrayed, it is one of the worst feelings you can endure. You don't feel betrayal from a stranger or even an ordinary acquaintance, but it is generally someone you hold dear in your heart, someone you never thought would betray you. The problem is that you don't take the time to really know a person before giving your trust to them, which opens the door for betrayal. Trust is something that should not be given so easily. Unfortunately, you ignore signs and important details that could keep you from being hurt. The caveat to all of this is that it may not have been that you put trust in this person; instead, because of their relationship to you, you expected to be able to trust them.

This excludes people who were betrayed by a parent, spouse, spiritual leader, or someone of influence; they didn't have a choice, since trusting in some people is a natural thing based on their relationship with us. Maybe you didn't count on them to come through for you on something, but you were disappointed because you loved and trusted them, and they let you down. Sometimes, you have expectations of people and have no clue they would betray you. When you go through an ordeal that is traumatic, caused by you trusting the wrong person, you may not want to trust anyone else again. When this occurs, you have to realize that you can't go through life not trusting anyone; you just have to be careful as to who you're willing to give your trust. Hurt is something that everyone wants to avoid, but pain in life is inevitable. The key to this is your response and reaction to the hurt. Okay, it's happened, and there's nothing you can do about it, but where do you go from there? I would like to think that you have what it takes to go forward, even after the betrayal, as well as going forward because of the betrayal.

You may not realize it, but love is connected to your trust. When you can't trust, you will struggle to love. Betrayal ruins something deep on the inside. Honestly, that type of hurt can last for years. The act of betrayal is often undetected, but it eventually has a great impact. People have taken their lives because of betrayal. The scarring that comes from betrayal is a lifelong remembrance; you don't forget these traumatic things, but their effects shouldn't last a lifetime. You have so much to live for; why give someone who mistreated you the victory over your life? Let the scarring serve as motivation, and overcome it. You can use that dark place in your life to bring light to your path and certainly to your future. What makes a success story is success. You can be that success story. You can be that person who dealt with adversity, but through the power of God and your faith and belief in yourself, you made it and turned it around in your favor.

When you make it, don't be afraid to throw it back in the devil's face. This is why I said earlier that trust issues cause TDS. Almost every day, I talk to people dealing with major trust issues, causing them to constantly struggle with relationships in their lives. I heard a saying that when a person shows you who they are, then believe it. Just remember: We all make mistakes, and sometimes a person's betrayal was just that, but don't be a fool, either. People who are truly sorry will show their remorse. Love them anyway. In this life, God requires us to have faith, and after we establish our faith and it becomes permanent, our faith should then develop into trust. Love can be ruined if you are unable to trust. The inability to love stems from a heart that is not able to trust or a heart that has been hurt by a past situation. Issues that destroy your ability to trust fill your heart with corrosion. TDS keeps so many people from going forward and progressing. Fear can cancel trust indefinitely. Fear is not of God; it's a weapon of the enemy to cause corrosion to destroy your faith and trust. The Bible states in Isaiah 54 and verse 17 that "no weapon formed against me shall prosper." People have so many things working against them that they become frightened by what they perceive as a negative outcome and then decide against change.

For most people, the lack of support from loved ones can further increase fear. When you feel that you are all alone, it becomes a struggle; indecisive thoughts may lead you to believe you cannot change the situation. You often look for someone you love to be your encouragement. What happens when they don't encourage you? What happens when they don't support your decision to change? You must first recall that the change is necessary, and you must remember who the change is for. You have to learn from your past mistakes in order to make better choices in life.

Sometimes, when you are going through changes and there seems to be no one supporting you, you must encourage yourself. I believe that I will make it because I have a Father in heaven who loves me and cares about me. When given a reason, I will assess the people in my life to determine their purpose in order to ensure that they belong in my circle. Some people may not be able to show love to you if they have never had love shown to them. They want to love but just don't know how. It feels bad when tough decisions arise but no one is around to support you. We all need someone in this life to be in our corner, but when there is no one there, we still must remember that God is always there. The past can cause your future to become corroded, but you can avoid this. I have seen corrosion start in a small area and eat away at the good and healthy areas until the entire object was corroded. Your heart is the same way, once corrosion sets in. You have so much hurt and pain left in your heart, until it spreads to your mind. Then, you can't see past the hurt, which causes you to hurt other people.

We live our lives in the heart of the past and accept the moment as being final. There is a word that comes to mind, *residue,* which means something remaining or left over. Most people have scars from past pains; this residue can be insurmountable at times, causing them to fear progress or change. You may often feel there's been so much damage to your psyche that you can't move ahead, but don't let it be so bad that you don't even try to make it better. You may think that you've tried so many times, but you seem to fall back into a valley experience. A valley experience is an analogy of being in a deep hole or rut. When God gives you a charge to change, he wants your entire heart and mind, but this is difficult when you have so much residue left behind. People have moved on, but because you're not ready for a change, the baggage you are carrying halts you. The analogy that comes to mind is that you have your luggage packed but are carrying it around and going nowhere. You have taken the time and packed the bags (years of stuff) but are not even going on a trip. Why pack your baggage? Why carry the luggage but don't unload it? If I'm going to carry around the baggage, eventually, I should look to put it down and unpack.

One sure trip that everyone must take when ready to put down their baggage is a trip to the altar of God. Psalm 55 states for us to cast all of our burdens upon him, and he will sustain you. It is so difficult to move ahead when you keep the reminder (residue) of your past hurts and fears in your forefront. When God gives you the charge to change, you must change the areas of your life that keep you from trusting him. The devil wants you to be unhappy for the rest of your life so you never experience peace or love of Christ in your heart. The one part of the body that is always under attack from the enemy is the heart. He wants you to harbor ill feeling, hurt, anger, jealousy, malice, and hatred in your heart. The enemy wants you to live in constant unhappiness and discouragement while not trusting so that you can't feel love, while making every attempt to hinder you from loving. When the enemy separates you from your faith, he is able to drive a wedge between your mind and your heart. Satan wants to control your thoughts so he then can control your life. Change is a major factor for the devil, who wants people to remain in fear and doubt; he knows he has no control over you unless you give it to him. The devil pushes you to make bad choices in your life in order to keep you bound in bad situations. A charge to change is about freedom and redemption, free to live and redeemed to be esteemed. To be esteemed, you must walk in freedom. To be esteemed, you must transform yourself into someone of importance; God wants us to know that we are important in his eyes. There are four steps to change: alteration, elimination, elevation, and celebration. The next chapter will discuss these steps.

Chapter 14

Principles of Your Process

Change is a process of alteration, elimination, elevation, and celebration. Patience is required for every step of change. When going through a tough time in life that lead to a change occurring, the alteration step is critical. I talk about this process of alteration at length because you must understand what needs to happen to go through a change. Alteration occurs after the initial task is defined. To alter something means to change or modify. Alteration requires reconstruction in your environment, habits, or thinking, and it can be a short- or long-term process. The difficulty with change is getting through the total process. You will find that endurance is not always easy. Many things occur when going through the alteration process, which calls for decision making and definitive choices. You will also have to adjust some things physically, mentally, and definitely spiritually. When I think of alterations, I think about something being removed, cut, or sewn. Maybe something in your life left, walked away, or was removed, but you have to decide where you go from there. Maybe you went through something that cut through you like a knife, where someone cut you deeply with their words or just stabbed you in the back. I say again that you still have to pick yourself up from there and decide where to go. You often struggle to pick up the pieces, but there has to be a mending process, in which love and trust are sewn back together, little by little.

Alterations are also done to make sure that something fits properly. Therefore, look at it like this: Some issues you endured required that you go through some altering so your life would be complete and fit you better. Reconstruction sometimes requires things to be torn completely down or built from scratch. I have a great example for this: Jeremiah 18 speaks about the potter and the clay. This is a great story of something that needs altering. The Bible said that the potter sat at his wheel molding a pot while the wheels turned, and all of a sudden, he realized the pot he had created had some defects. He decided to remake the pot. The potter realized that remaking it was the best course of action so that what he created would be in the best condition when completed.

This may relate to your life; some people may have treated you badly or mishandled your love, trust, and care. There are times when you're not able to start over or rebuild, but when that moment comes, it has to be embraced because something that was faulty can be made again. The Bible says that the man who made the pot noticed the defects as he look at his creation. In his altering, the potter saw some things that need to be removed. God wants us to be healed and free from burdens, but we have to have peace and patience when he is remaking the situation to fit his expectations. We should not look like what we've gone through. We should want to look as the potter wants us to look: whole, without any defects. Alteration may call for minor changes or major ones. Altering your lifestyle may simply mean starting over. It's not always easy to start over, but sometimes it's necessary. Therefore, if *alteration* means to "change," then we must understand that *change* means "to alter." In life, we go through physical change more than any other change. Everything about the meaning of change denotes alteration. It takes confidence when trying to change some things in your life.

One of the definitions of *change* that captures my attention is "to undergo transformation and transition." Change is transformation. When going through a change in your life, it's inevitable that transformation will occur. When you think about the word *transformation*, it makes you think about starting out a certain way but growing into something else or manifesting into a different object. The root word for transformation is *transform*, which means "the changing of outward form or structure." For instance, it can be something as simple as changing jobs or as complex as ending a long-term relationship. It may have started out a certain way, but now it's time for it to evolve into something different. The job may have been a place of comfort, but now it has changed into a different role.

You may go from working in a uniform to working in a suit. In either situation, change is required.

Relationships can also effect change. You may have been in a good relationship, but then all of a sudden, the relationship ends on a bad note. This could cause you to go through a transformation. If it was a good relationship, then your outer structure may go from being happy all the time to sad. You will be transformed into something different. Transformation may be difficult, but the transition is sometimes even harder to endure. Sometimes, things occur that are beyond your control, and the transition into that place of change is extremely tough. It's tough to leave a job you liked or a person you loved so much, but something has initiated the change, and now you have to venture ahead into a place without that security blanket. One thing that is evident is that we have trouble leaving a comfortable situation.

Transition means "passage from one stage or place to another." This is a powerful statement because you go through many stages in life, and unfamiliar territory can be scary. The sad reality is that some people get stuck and never make the transition. Transitioning must be propelled by confidence and belief that you will successfully move from one state to the next. Even in transition, you are still going through transformation. You have to keep reminding yourself that prayer is a powerful tool to use when going through changes and transitions in life. As I stated earlier in the book, prayer and belief in God have brought me through many trials, changes, and situations. Sometimes, times of change can get so frustrating, they bring you to tears, but praying to God can restore your strength and rebuild the confidence you need to get through them. When I received Jesus Christ as my Lord and Savior, I found a way to get through tough periods of my life. To tell the truth, going through transformations and transitions can hurt.

Jesus said in John 16, verses 20 through 22, "I tell you the truth, you will weep and mourn over what is going to happen to me, but the world will rejoice and you will grieve, but your grief will suddenly turn to wonderful joy. It will be like a woman suffering the pains of labor. When her child is born, her anguish gives way to joy because she has brought a new baby into the world. So you have sorrow now, but I will see you again; then you will rejoice, and no one can rob you of that joy" (NLT). In order to get to the blessing, you sometimes must go through the pain.

During the time of pain, there was crying and hurt, but Jesus said it would turn into joy. Sometimes, you have to endure the pain, but may only last a short while. Therefore, change may hurt you sometimes, but you have to continue to press forward to get to that place you seek. In order for a woman to give birth to a baby, which is one of the most blessed moments to occur in life, there is a level of pain that takes place before the moments of joy and happiness. Even though her body was altered, the package on the inside was worth the pain that had to be endured. One key element when change occurs is for people to feel confident and know they have the power to change. Circumstances may dictate the change, but God will give the charge to change. You go through heartaches and pains without understanding the meaning, but you can decide whether you get the better of the problem or allow the problem to get the better of you.

The Bible refers to the devil as the enemy, and he most certainly upholds that title. The enemy wants to keep us in bad positions and bad places in our lives. Alteration was the first step of change, but there are three more that we must process in order to deal with change. The second step is elimination. Some people, places, and situations must be eliminated in order to bring about change. The elimination process is more difficult than the alteration process because it requires cutting off and getting rid of unwanted excess. In the elimination process, some familiar things can be negative, and they need to be discarded. For instance, if you have a habit of chemical dependence, you must eliminate the things that lead you back into the habit. People often get addicted to substances because of stress, loss, hurt, or frustrations of life. Then, it would take you to do something different to be able to change. In order to eliminate the things causing the dependence, you would have to get rid of anything that is a constant reminder that leads to your struggle, like spending money on drugs and alcohol. Some things happen to us that we cannot physically eliminate, but sometimes things are mental. It may take changing an environment. It may be as simple as surrounding yourself with positive people, who keep you encouraged and speak hope into your life. When you have the wrong people around you, it can have a major impact when dealing with the trials of life.

The step of elimination may require you to let go of something you hold dear to your heart. *Eliminate* means "to get rid of." The word *elimination* refers to something that's become unimportant and irrelevant. Think about it like this: Why would you keep something that's no longer relevant or important? Why waste time and energy on someone who is not a plus to your life? It's time to change. I get it that most people do it because of familiarity, but what good is that if you're not happy? Don't your feelings matter? The elimination process of change is a difficult one because you have so many emotions tied to things that were once meaningful, but something happened, and it has lost its value. The one thing that should never lose its value is the meaning of your life. When you think about elimination, you should think about what in your life you need to get rid of in order to move to the next step of this process. I truly believe that everyone has some things that need to be removed or eliminated from their lives. Everyone has to examine every situation that they face in order to see what's causing a hindrance. Sometimes, the people we love may work against our plan and God's plan.

The devil will always be our adversary and will not stop until he ruins God's plan in our lives. We have to get rid of anything that is opposed to our destiny. Sometimes, you have to disconnect from disconnected people and connect yourself to connected people. I'm not saying remove everything meaningful just because you don't see a benefit, but just people you know are hindering you and your progress. We all want to see progress, but most of the time, we aren't willing to complete the process. It may be that one thing that's keeping you from something great, but fear of letting it go stops you. I encourage you to reach the levels in your life that you are destined to reach. You should grow in every area of your life, every day.

The third phase in the change process is the elevation step. When you've made drastic changes to your culture, which is mainly your thinking and your environment, an elevation should take place. Everyone should elevate their lives. *Elevation* means something that rises. It is time for you to rise. It is meant for you to rise up and go higher than you could have ever imagined. When you deal with trials and tribulations, you must focus on rising above and reaching a new level. Elevation is not going to happen if there is no drive to elevate. You can stay in a rut for so long that you stop thinking there's growth beyond that place. If the truth be told, we've all been in a rut, but there's always an out to being in that place.

There is a lesson to be learned in everything we face in life, whether the lesson is easy or difficult to learn.

I remember studying about eagles and was amazed at how they fit this topic of elevation. The first thing you have to realize is that when you are about to elevate, you have to be connected to the right people and connected to the right place. Connecting yourself to the right people will put you in a class of people with vision like an eagle. Eagles don't hang with chickens. Eagles may be birds, but they are clearly a different type of bird. A chicken can only fly a few feet in the air, and for only a short time. Chickens have feathers, like eagles, but that similarity doesn't put them in the same class. A chicken dwells more on land because of its limitations, but an eagle soars into the clouds. An eagle nests in places difficult for humans to reach.

An eagle has certain traits that people should emulate. I will share with you some of their distinct characteristics that will motivate you to want elevation and want it quickly. First, eagles have keen vision; they can see three miles in the air, looking down at an object that is smaller than a mouse. People have to be able to trust in the things they see and not be fooled by the objects being viewed. We should be better at seeing things ahead. We should have a vision, which means looking for what is to come. The one thing I can take away from the differences between an eagle and chicken is that I may come from the same place as someone else, but our destiny will differ. An eagle keeps balance between other eagles. He flies higher than others to view the landscape and find what it desires. Eagles are known for flying to great heights to get where they want to go. Eagles fly high because that's their nature, how they were made. Second, an eagle is patient, focused, and driven, which are qualities we need to succeed.

As another example, an automaker like Honda will design many kinds of cars so they can reach every class of people. The more expensive carmakers will only produce a few models because they only intend to reach the upper class. A carmaker like Mercedes will change only as needed in order to build their brand with quality vehicles, and they don't believe in cheapening their brand by just throwing something together. This type of thinking is for people who may not be able to afford it at the time, but with motivation and focus, they will push to get to a place of elevation; they will be able to get in this class and sustain at this level.

That's why eagles won't lower their beliefs and become bottom dwellers. They were made to soar, and so were you.

Finally, an eagle loves storms with strong winds. When I read this, I thought it was strange. Why would anyone embrace being in a storm? Why would anyone look for a storm? Scientists say that eagles view it as a time to rest. Wow. Rest in a storm? Scientists say that when a storm comes, eagles fly even higher and use the winds to soar without flapping their wings. In a storm, eagles just glide; they don't have to exert energy flapping their wings. They just ride the waves of the winds; they love it because the storms push them higher, and the higher they go, the more rest they experience.

I take from this that sometimes, it's about how you look at a situation. When you have storms (troubles) in your life, you should see that this is a moment to rise and elevate. Everything happens for a reason; therefore, why not elevate from it? It is your time to rest and soar because elevation is meant for you.

The fourth principle of the change process is celebration. We will party for birthdays, anniversaries, holidays, and other special days that we have grown accustomed to acknowledging. We'd rather have fun instead of having a sure future. You overcome so many obstacles in your life; why not celebrate that moment of victory, when you personally know how tough it was for you to make it? I celebrate the victories I've accomplished when everything seemed stacked against me. The celebration part of this process is worth every moment of struggle, but it highlights the reward and success of completing the process. I believe you should turn up (the right way) when you've elevated to your next level. This is a time for you to look back and reflect that you did it and made it with the help of God, prayer, and faith.

After you've altered some areas of your life and then realized that some elimination was needed, the elevation to your new level has now come, and then it's time for you to celebrate. Celebrate because you endured the process and you realized that change is necessary.

Chapter 15

Your World Is Not Falling Apart

Throughout the years, when people went through spiritual warfare, I would hear them say that their world was falling apart. In warfare, things are destroyed, but there's an opportunity for rebuilding that comes after a war. Your mind is the world that you feel is crumbling, but actually, God is reconstructing your mind to be more like his.

When I consider what it takes to begin the process of change, I think about patience, desire, perseverance, will, and passion. You need patience when a situation is changing. Your desire can drive change; it takes a strong desire to move toward change. When changing, you must persevere through the discouragement and fight to make the right decisions. It takes a strong will to be determined not to give up or feel that change is hopeless. Victory is won when your passion to change is greater than your fear of change. The one factor that is relevant in the entire change process is having enough inner strength to make the tough decisions. As I think about change, a high level of confidence plays a major part in the transition of changes. The course of change is altered if I think that my willpower is not strong enough.

Whenever someone tries to begin a new life, obstacles seem to appear; many obstacles seem so tall that they lose focus on the course. In this life, you have to stop looking at things through your eyes and begin to look at things through the eyes of Christ. The way you look through the eyes of Christ is in constant reading of the Word of God, meditation, fasting, and much prayer. These factors are so important in obtaining strength as well as the peace needed during difficult situations. Everyone has the ability to pray; however, it takes more than words. It takes a relationship with God. People can only speak about their own experiences, but my testimony is that I've been able to overcome many trying obstacles in my life, and God was there all the time.

Some people perceive that God is cruel or doesn't exist, but that's not true. God cares about you and everything pertaining to your life. Some people perceive that God isn't listening to us. They doubt that he actually cares when certain things don't work in our favor. There are a few questions that are always pertinent, such as, Did we consult God? What was the outcome? Why did God allow it to happen? We often question God when things don't go our way. God always provide us with direction and instruction. We can't expect him to give us instruction when we are not in his will. It is not God's will for us to suffer. The Bible says that "the steps of a good man are ordered by the LORD" (Psalm 37:23 KJV). When God ordains your steps, he often takes you through places where you're uncomfortable, which can make you frustrated. You can get frustrated because the Word of God is true, and you may not understand your purpose. You often try so hard to make changes in your life; when it's not going your way, and you don't understand your purpose, you may question your purpose. Throughout life, you will experience moments of frustration over finances, marital problems, family issues, job situations, and other internal issues, but you shouldn't have the spirit of fear or give up when dealing with these trials. People mostly struggle over financial and family issues. There are so many people who are searching for answers, but they become frustrated over the time it can take to get an answer.

Change is necessary, but most people give up because of their frustration. Before you get frustrated, remember this: You need to think about whether you consulted God or not. If you consult God in everything you do, then most situations will be easier to handle (I said "most situations," due to the fact that nothing is easy all the time). God places you in certain situations to see if you're willing to listen to him, trust him, humble yourself, and live according to his Bible. When you do not fulfill his commandments, you may find yourself struggling in certain areas. The word *frustration* means the state of being frustrated, and a deep, chronic sense of insecurity and dissatisfaction arising from unresolved problems or unfulfilled needs. If you look at the meaning of the word *frustration*, people often struggle with insecurities, which gives birth to fear. The devil knows that if he can get you in a fearful state, you won't be confident enough to make a change. The enemy thinks that getting you frustrated is one of the best tools he has to halt or destroy the path leading to change.

To be honest, we've all struggled with insecurities, which led to moments of being frustrated. When I was growing up, I was often frustrated because of something changing in my life. I have my share of testimonies, which were the result of some changes that occurred in my life. When I was about ten or eleven, the doctors discovered that I had a degenerative disease in my bones (soft bones) caused by lack of calcium. The hip bone that connects to the hip socket on the left side of my hip had slipped out of place; the doctors inserted three long pins in my hip bone to keep the bone in place with the socket.

After the doctor performed the surgery, while I was in the recovery room, they discovered they had used the wrong pins; they had to rush me back to surgery to remove them and put in the correct pins. My parents were so angry because they saw their son having to go through all of this and suffer with all of the pain. I literally had to learn to walk all over again. I went through many days of pain and anguish. It was really hard adjusting to the pins in my hip. At the beginning, I was pretty much confined to bed. When I went through rehab, I had to use a walker for about three months, then I was on crutches for a few more months. My home life and school life were altered dramatically. I had to have help to get around at school and at home. The doctors didn't think I'd be able to play sports, but I held out hope that I could be an athlete. The doctor stated that only time would tell, depending on how the hip healed.

My hip turned out fine, but at times there were minor issues of pain. After a while, I was able to get back to living a normal life as a youth. When things are going good in your life, you're often unprepared for bad things that may occur. You should look with compassion at others who may be dealing with ailments or other deficiencies. Though my life was altered briefly, I was still able to recover, and I thought I'd never have to deal with that situation again. Just about the time where I was feeling better about myself, the very next year, I was running outside, chasing a dog while it was raining, and I fell and broke my leg in two, right above the knee. I broke my leg so bad that the bone was bulging against my thigh, looking like it was about to burst through my flesh. As I revisit this in my mind, I remember lying on the ground, screaming and seeing my bone about to break through my skin.

Mom ran out of the house with a scared and hurt look on her face because she witnessed me falling as she watched out of the window. She ran out of the house and saw the condition of my leg. Due to my size, she couldn't pick me up, and my dad wasn't at home. My mom called next door over to my grandmother's house for my uncle Boone, who was a bodybuilder and a wrestler at the time. He was definitely strong enough as well as being the only one who could lift me up off of the ground. Uncle Boone put me in the van, and my mom rushed me to the hospital. All I could think as I was crying was that here I was, dealing with a bad leg all over again.

Within a few years, I had two major surgeries on my left leg. In a two-year span, I spent over sixteen months on crutches or using a walker. When I was about twelve years of age, I thought I would become this great football player because I had the build and the speed for my size, but all it took was just one day, and my life changed, which caused me to have to adjust once again. I broke my leg again, this time above the knee. I knew that this pretty much sealed my fate of ever becoming a ballplayer. The doctor said I'd never be able to play football or any sports. He told me that playing sports could make me even more of a cripple, that I may need a wheelchair or some other support device. I was now considered a cripple in my eyes, and everyone else's. This was a devastating blow to a twelve-year-old boy who desired to play sports. This situation not only stopped me from playing football, but I could not play any sports, even in my leisure time.

From 1985 to 1986, I was on crutches and a walker for about six months, and I had to rehab the next six months. After rehabbing, it was difficult to stay encouraged, and I spent many days staring out my window in frustration because I felt that I shouldn't be going through this type of change. I sat many days unhappy about being young and physically hurt, looking out my window at all my neighborhood friends, who were able to run around and play. I had a hard time understanding why I had to go through this, and it led to many periods of discouragement and anger. I cried every day, wishing I had another chance to be able to do the things those other twelve-year-olds could do.

My grandmother tried to keep my spirits up, but I still couldn't understand. Many days, I just lay in bed, listening to the kids playing outside and knowing that I couldn't join them. I missed basketball, hide-and-seek, running through the woods, and catching locusts. I was not ready for my life to change in this way, but at a young age, I had to deal with change. I can remember feeling worthless because I couldn't do anything for myself while I was hurt. After the incident with my hip, I missed many days of school. Upon returning to school, I needed someone to help me get off the bus, get to my classes, get back on the bus, and even help me go to the bathroom. I was a proud young teenager, and this was hard to deal with. As a young person enduring trauma and change, I didn't realize that God gave me good friends and family to help me cope with being handicapped. On my first day back at school, they asked me which of my friends could help me get from class to class. This was so hard; just a short time prior, I was able to get around on my own, and now I couldn't because of my handicap.

In another blow, school officials said they wanted me to leave class five to ten minutes earlier than everyone else, so I could avoid the crowds in the halls. This was totally embarrassing; not only was I crippled, but I was being treated like a cripple. I was at the lowest point of my life. The few minutes in the halls were a time to briefly chat and goof off with friends, but I was unable to even do that anymore. When you go through something that alters your whole life, it's hard to see the good things because you become distracted with the bad things you've endured. I was a kid but felt that I was losing an important part of my life.

I had wonderful friends who helped me, but I felt that I should be healthy and get around on my own without needing anyone's help. Many people didn't understand why I felt to insignificant. I was so bitter, angry, and unhappy that I often wondered why I had to travel this road. Physical change can be as devastating as mental change. I often wonder what my life would've been like if I hadn't gone through these situations as a youth. When I lost what I thought was the ability to be a normal child, I began faking happiness when others were around, but all the time, I was crying on the inside. Many years went by with me feeling inferior and insecure. Unfortunately, change is not just for people of a certain age, but it is inevitable; everyone has to deal with change. I can remember spending many hours with my grandma, who was my primary care person due to my mom and dad having to work. I cried for many days because I felt this change in my life was too hard. I remember thinking that only elderly people used walkers, but now I had to use one too.

These were the hardest two years of my life. During rehab, I had to learn how to walk all over again. I felt that there was nothing good about life and that I would be a cripple for my entire life. I was totally discouraged; my self-esteem, confidence, hope, and happiness were dead. My grandma always told me that God had a plan for my life, but as a young person, I didn't understand. I thought that football was my future, but I was about to find out my purpose.

There's an old saying, "When it rains, it pours." For me, I really believed it to be true; while recovering from my leg injuries, I had seizures, which caused me to become blind; I also developed kidney and lung problems. All I could think was, *Why me? What could happen next?* I was in the hospital, crying out to my mom because I couldn't see. I was physically blind and terrified that I would never see again. During the same period, my kidneys and lungs were not functioning properly; they shut down. The doctors didn't know what was happening.

I can truly say now that it was God and the prayers of my parents and other believers that brought me through. The doctors believed that all the things that were happening to me were caused by seizures. I often wondered what was wrong with me to where I had to endure these trials and tribulations. As you can imagine, I had so many fears, doubts, and insecurities due to my many different conditions. I had leg issues, and on top of that, all of these other sicknesses popping up on me. Being blind was scary and far worse in my mind than my leg issue.

I should have been thankful and not worried about the other issues after coming through something like blindness, but I didn't feel that way. How could a kid like me lose his sight? Many times during these years, I asked, "Why me?" When you're a young person, you don't understand things like this. I do thank God that I had parents who believed and certainly had the faith.

This was the scariest moment in my life, and the doctor had no answers. To be blind and not know when or if I would ever see again, I became hysterical. I just wanted to die. I had already dealt with so much up until that moment, and I just wondered what more could happen to me. I feel that I've been through so much that I know there's a purpose to my life.

Eventually, after a week or so, my sight did come back. Being a kid, I then defaulted back to focusing on my leg condition. As people do all the time, when you overcome a tough situation, instead of being grateful, you go back to focusing on the negatives. As I grew older, my leg condition got better, and I just had to learn how to make it work for me. I became determined to disprove what the doctor stated. I began to do more and started going outside with the rest of the kids in the neighborhood, just so I could share their enjoyment. I knew I'd never play school ball, but at least I could play around the neighborhood. I couldn't run around like the rest of the kids, but I was determined to come close.

As I advanced in school, we had to select classes that we needed to graduate, and from the ninth to the twelfth grade, I selected a physical education class just so I could do some type of activity such as basketball or volleyball. My legs began to get stronger; the doctor had told me that my leg issues were due to low calcium. I can say that I worked as hard as I could over the next few years and eventually began to do some of the physical things I thought I'd never be able to do. Even though this was a great accomplishment for me, I was still bitter because of what I had been through. I truly believe now that God knew what he was doing because he wanted me to serve him. I lived for many years in frustration and anger because of the changes that I went through.

When God speaks change to take place, it will happen because he has a much bigger plan in mind. Yes, my youth was marred with hurt, pain, disappointment, and anger, but now that I've accepted God in my life, he has truly been there every step of the way. Jesus began his ministry at the age of twelve, and God started me on mine at the age of twelve (wow). I could not have made it through without the love God has given to me and the people he gave for me when going through a difficult change. Some people don't have loved ones to help them through, but God proves that he is everything to us, and he is our ultimate loved one.

As I grew up, I found that I could still set goals and achieve them. One goal I set was that I could run, play ball, and have a somewhat normal childhood. As the years went by and with some hard work, I was able to run pretty good, and I became a decent neighborhood ballplayer. When in high school, I used to go to the gym and play ball with some players on the basketball team. I ran up and down that court just like anyone else and enjoyed the opportunity that God gave me and the strength he gave me to do it. This was a great moment of achievement for me because I was adapting to change and making the best out of the situation.

The crowning moment of redemption came when I went to Arkansas State; the football coach saw me playing basketball in the gym and thought I was a possible recruit candidate visiting the campus. When he learned that I was a student and not a recruit, he asked me if I was interested in being a walk-on on the football team. I told him about my hip issue and asked if he could he guarantee that if I got hit in my hip, I wouldn't be a cripple for the rest of my life. He said that he couldn't guarantee something like that. I declined his offer because I knew my limitations, but it felt so good to be wanted because of the trials of my youth and everything that I dealt with regarding my leg injury.

My point to this is that change happens voluntarily or involuntarily. For whatever reason, please know that some changes will happen and are necessary, but you have to be patient until you learn your purpose. I was able to stop hating everything and everyone and begin to move forward to the change God had for me. I learned that when you're going through a difficult change, you must believe in yourself and trust in God. If you don't think you can make it, then most times you won't. If you're lacking confidence in yourself, most situations will be more difficult to handle. We look for people to be our power supply, but there is only one person who can be our power supply, and his name is Jesus Christ. People believe in humans more, and they don't believe in God. It may very well be that the person you believe in believes in God, which gets them through tough times and everyday living. They tend to look for people to be their life support. In this life, we are often disappointed by people because we believe them to be more than what they really are. When God has given you a charge to change, that is a personal request, and the only thing people can do for you is give you support.

In the event that you don't have anyone to support you, then you have to remain encouraged and get through it on your own, with assistance from God. Hurt people hurt people, and when people have never experienced love, they are not the best models to show love. When people are badly hurt, they become immune to hurt but combative to love. These types of people can be destructive and volatile. We all want to be loved and need to feel loved. This person may not be a bad person, but they may be bad for you at that time. People need to heal first before they move on to someone else. This type of person may not embrace a friend or companion if pain has always been the norm. You just have to watch and be careful because the backlash of what someone else has been wounded by may very well cause hurt and pain to you. I encourage you that if you've ever been hurt or wounded, work on yourself so you can be a help to others. You don't want to find someone you really care about, only to lose them because of the past.

I had to admit that I had some issues in order to get help and change that part of my life that was not healthy in relationship to others. You may not mean to hurt others, but the reality is that you do when you don't get yourself together. Even though many people don't believe in God, he still believes in us. The believers were not always believers, but God still provided. He is so patient with us that he gives us time to make the decisions we need to make in order for us to experience a dynamic change in our lives. I guarantee that there is not a person in the world who has not experienced change in some area of their lives. In the Bible, Christ left his place in heaven, which was on the right hand of the Father (God), and positioned himself in a fleshly body to come and give us hope, life, peace, and an eternal home. You won't find a king or a prince who would give up their riches to become a pauper, but Christ was willing, and he did it for all of us. He chose to change from being in his heavenly environment into an environment of sin and pain. From the moment Christ entered into this world, he went through many changes, but the end result was for all of us to gain victory and have an eternal home.

You can lose out on so many things in life because of your reluctance to change. There is an old saying, "When the going gets tough, the tough gets going." This cliché can be viewed in a positive or a negative manner. At times, you must all know that when things in life come upon you or when things get extremely tough, you must evaluate the situation, determine the severity, and decide on what actions to take. The cliché should be taken that when difficult situations arise, we must get tough to make it through. Sometimes, being tough means walking away, and other times, it means making a stand, which is still synonymous of change. In most cases, you have to leave someone when you're going through tough times. Each individual must determine the severity of the issue and assess what would happen if they stayed in a negative place or remain with a negative person.

The one constant in most people's life is that the idea of change may stem from a bad incident. After determining the seriousness of the issue, you must then decide on the actions that must occur. I can't see someone who is abused thinking that it's okay to continue in a relationship of abuse, but you never know what goes through a person's mind. Maybe fear is a driving factor to deny change from a situation like that. It could be possible to get so used to a situation that you just settle, even if you're being mistreated. The only thing I can say is that no matter what, you have to value yourself, and it's not worth putting your hands on someone or someone putting their hands on you. I can say that change is definitely necessary for situations of abuse, but it takes that person to get enough of that and decide to step out and change. It is not always an easy thing to do, but it's a necessary thing to do in order to be happy and live.

It's hard to comprehend how someone could think that God doesn't expect great things in our lives. You think that God doesn't care about you when certain things happen to us, but this is certainly not true. God gave his only begotten Son so that we'd have everlasting life and an eternal home. When change is necessary, you must decide what is more important and what direction you must take. When deciding on what steps should be taken, a well-thought-out plan must be formed. When deciding on your next step, you must first stay strong and rebuke your fears. When the going gets tough, the tough should call on and trust in the one who will always make a way. God will never leave you or forsake you. When you've done all you can do, then keep your head up and stand tall.

Through the rough times in life, you face many challenges of change. I've been in many situations where certain factors determined change.

We often focus on the difficult decisions. Let's discuss some of the difficult decisions you're faced with. The most important example of making difficult decisions is in the area of relationships. Relationships are the most common source of change in your life. You may be in a relationship that is unhealthy or that turned bad over time. This is a topic of concern for us as individuals, but most importantly, this is a major topic of concern for God. The Bible says that God is a jealous God. It also tells you not to put anyone before him. You often give more to your natural relationships than to your relationship with God. You can focus so much time and energy on the relationship that you form an enormous bond that isn't easy to break. There are times when people are hurt or mistreated but are blinded by time they invested in the relationship and decide to just stay. Some people stay in negative relationships due to the connection and bond to the other individual. You can give so much of yourself that you lose yourself in the relationship. Most people give their mate an identity and lose their own. They build up the other person but are torn down themselves. So many people in relationships lose the total essence of who they are and what they're all about.

When there is a need for change, you should look at and evaluate everything about your relationships. When you lose your identity, you lose your vision (not your natural vision, your spiritual vision). A relationship should not be the cause for identity theft, but giving up who you are is like allowing a thief to come in and take it away. Identity theft can be costly. It can take a long time to correct. Don't ever lose yourself.

If you're in a negative relationship, then over time, there will be a loss of identity, if your focus is not on change. Many people who are in negative (or dare I say bad) relationships forget about their hopes and dreams and live their lives according to their partner's view of how they should live. Identity theft is a situation where someone steals your name and uses it for personal gain. They take on and control your identity and financial accounts. Just like some relationships, people who are close to us can control your identity. After you lose yourself, then change is much harder to embrace, and you stay bound, which causes you to give up, be unhappy, or feel that this is the best you can do.

Every relationship is different, and some are really good, but what makes relationships positive are the people and the environment. It takes effort from both parties to make it fulfilling. If one person is not willing to keep the relationship healthy, then all of a sudden, change may be necessary. You should always have high expectations for what you want in life, or you'll find yourself wanting a change in your environment; you may find yourself wasting many years without fulfilling your purpose. A relationship without purpose or expectation can be uncomfortable and cause a lot of pain. Positive relationships should be desired and health, not despised and unwanted.

It's not just up to you if your relationship has purpose, meaning, and promise. If the situation has no promise, then change is necessary. I always tell people that if someone isn't adding to your life, then it's time to subtract them from your life. In a relationship, there should be addition and multiplying and not subtraction or division. Change can add and multiply to your situation, but the fear of change can subtract and divide you and your life. Change may not be easy, but I repeat from the first paragraph that change is necessary.

Most people look for a different perspective or outlook in life. Self-esteem can drive you to victory or failure. There is not a person on this earth who wants to be a failure; no one wants to fail. Self-esteem can be a mental stumbling block if you're not careful. When you lack confidence, you just may build a foundation for disappointment and regret. People often look at the negatives in their lives because that's the picture that was painted by someone else. You must know that God made you victorious; there's no problem that you can't overcome. You are more than an overcomer, according to the Word of God, but you must believe you can do it with him on your side. God is your truth, your way, and your life. The Bible states that the Word is a lamp unto my feet and a light unto my path. When your self-esteem has taken a major hit, the Word of God is an instant pick-me-up. I've met many people who feel they can't do a certain thing only because they lack confidence. Low self-esteem is an enemy of confidence and attacks it every time it gets an opportunity. Self-esteem can give you a boost, but not when it's low. In this life, there are going to be some things that you desire, but they may not work in your favor. The key to success is being able to go through failure, but not stay in it. Success is only achieved through endurance and perseverance. If your esteem is too low, you may give up or turn back.

When change is necessary, there has to be a strong will and desire to achieve it. Most successful people will tell you they failed a few times before achieving success. You can't allow previous failures to detour you from the success of a positive change. Most people will give up if a task is not successful the first time. Success is gained through a continual repetition of effort. Honestly, some changes will downright scare you, but failure should scare you more. God made you better than you live. He made you to enjoy life but never said there would be no tests or trials. Change is sometimes a goal, but can be a determining factor with the result. I say it that way because sometimes changing is a challenge, but when you make it through the change, the result is victory. You often think that you're in difficult situations, but there is always someone out there who is going through much tougher things. How does it feel to be able to see through your eyes your whole life, only to have your eyesight taken because of illness? How about waking up one day and being blind in both eyes because of a seizure? This would be a major change to anyone's life. As I stated earlier in the book, this happened to me and could happen to you as well, if circumstances dictated. Your life is filled with changes, which occur quite often. Every living being goes through some type of change. You have your ups and downs in life, but change is a reoccurring thing that can pose a challenge. Challenges are tough, but God is tougher. When the going gets tough is when he gets going. In chapter 18 of Genesis, God asked a question, but in reality it wasn't a question. He asked, "Is anything too hard for GOD?" (KJV). He knows that there is nothing too hard for him. We think some situations are impossible, but the word *impossible* does not exist in the spiritual realm. Matthew 19:26 states, "With God, all things are possible (KJV).

I just want to go back a moment to make this point. When I was about twelve years old, around the time that I was nursing a broken hip, I had a seizure and was unable to see. For the next twelve years or so, I can truly say that I was depressed and unhappy; I felt that I was losing out on so many things that other people was able to enjoy. Though God restored my eyesight, I was angry for such a long time and couldn't understand why these things had happened to me. For years, I was hurting so bad on the inside because I felt that I should be in the NFL, making lots of money and enjoying life. The reality is that even if I had not become ill, there's no guarantee I would have played professional ball. In this life, many people hide their inadequacies and inferiority complexes. My self-esteem took a major hit because I felt that I was a cripple, and the doctors told me that in so many words. I needed someone to help me for several years. I had to depend on people helping me get around at home and at school. I needed help on simple things such as bringing me a cup of water. I felt people were just having pity on the helpless, crippled little boy. I cried many nights and felt that I had no purpose in this life. I lacked confidence and felt sorry for myself for such a long time. I saw people who were crippled and used to wonder how they kept themselves motivated and happy. I became so angry that I allowed it to control me, to the point of never really being happy growing up.

Once you allow anger inside you, it will grow into this humongous weight, and your entire life will evolve around your anger. I felt like an outcast because of my physical deficiencies. It was an awful time in my life; I needed people at home, church, and school to do things for me because I couldn't do anything for myself. I had to just wait until someone helped me. I felt no one in this world understood the changes I was going through. As I look at life today, I often wonder where I'd be if I didn't go through those circumstances. Little did I know that God had a plan for my life. The one change that I know God had purposed for my life was to deal with my pride. As a little boy, you'd think that there wouldn't be much pride, but God looks into your destiny and removes all things that could hinder your progress. I still went through a period where I was full of pride, but when you endure turmoil, it develops humility.

The charge to change that was ordained by God in my life started when I was very young. In life, we look at certain situations as being bad, but the Bible says that God meant for my life to be good and abundant. In every situation I've gone through, I didn't always see that good could come from it. I didn't always think positive, but as time went by, I began to see that life was waiting for me, and I couldn't keep waiting for life. I figured that I could always be bitter and unhappy, or I could adjust to my situation and live the life that God had given me. It took many years to see the path he had for me. God knew that if I went down certain roads, I wouldn't return.

I continue to strive for better changes, and I know that if I pursue positive roads, my life will evolve into a position that most pleases God. You try so hard in life to figure out why certain things happen to you, but he knows your expected end; you should figure out why you make certain decisions that lead you into peculiar situations. There is no one on earth who can say that they've never had to change from a situation. We wrestle with ourselves when it comes to changing. Many people live their lives according to a maybe, an assumption, or a distorted view. You can see the negatives before you reflect on the positives. Once you have viewed the negative, your mind should not shift to negativity. People often give up instead of holding out until the end.

Change requires great inner strength and patience. It will be difficult at times, but with perseverance, you can make it through the change. Change requires faith, stability, and a positive attitude to make it through the difficult times that come with changing. Remember: One of the meanings of *change* is to modify. When going through a change, you have to make deliberate and definite modifications. Modifying helps make the basic changes in order to serve a new end. This meaning was so profound and necessary for change. You must make wholesale changes to your life in order to give it a better outcome. When you make the necessary changes in your life, you have a far greater chance at success. Some areas of change only require a minimal amount of reconstruction. Some things in your life have gone on too long and need to be changed. If you get excited about where you want your life to go and dig deep and make the necessary modifications, change could lead to a successful result. If you're not able to do the things you could do in the past, you have to adjust the way you handle things. Every day, you have to adjust or adapt, which can mean getting rid of some stuff.

The first thing to remember is that you must always look at your attitude and the way you think. If your attitude is negative, the change will be seen as negative. If there is an unwillingness to change, then the need for change becomes a daunting challenge. Change has to start and end with self before it can actually happen. You have to make up your mind that change is needed; it must be what you want. Sometimes, you just have to be determined and driven to make change happen. Change can be forced upon you, but usually, that is in a negative way. The best scenario is for you to see the benefits of change. Your habits can also determine change. Habits can be anything physical or mental. Habits can include people and places. Habits will affect choices and outcomes. As people, we all have certain habits, whether we know it or not. Habits can be irritating but harmless. When looking at the aspect of changing, habits play an important role. History can determine your habits.

When God gives you a charge to change, you must break your old habits. Some people have been hurt so often that they become used to the pain. This starts a cycle where they come to expect it to continue. The continual cycle of hurt and being hurt develops into a habit. There is an old cliché: "Old habits are hard to break." This is a fairly true statement. It is not easy breaking away or changing from an old habit, but it is definitely possible. Habits form when there is a repeated occurrence, but breaking them occurs when a decisive mind breaks the action. Habits can be very damaging to your perspective and can hinder change. The longer drug addicts indulge in their habit, the longer it takes to change. By the time they realize they need to change, it could be too late.

Death is a last resort for changing. I have heard many cases where someone took too long from changing, and death was their outcome. God knows what areas need changing in your life, but the sad part is that many people don't have a relationship with him to be able to receive warning. I know for a fact that God exists, and he communicates with his people through the Holy Spirit. The Bible states that "the Holy Spirit maketh intercession for us" (KJV). The Spirit of God intercedes with Christ on our behalf. We must position ourselves to receive teachings from the Bible (Basic Instructions Before Leaving Earth).

My habits should not have control over me, but rather I should have control over my habits. Many times, you continue on a certain path because it's familiar. People often say, "It's a habit." They need to realize that if a habit causes discomfort, disappointment, or pain, then that door needs to open to change. You look at the obvious habits such as drugs and alcohol, but there are many other habits that can be life-changing and life-altering. Habits can cause the loss of friendships, resources, health, and life. Habits shouldn't limit your potential, nor should it cause you to regress in any area of your life. Habits are definitely an opportunity for change. When you have a relationship with God, he will point out the bad habits you need to get over. Many people have lost relationships because of a habit. In some cases, a habit broke up a family or a serious relationship. Habits such as chemical addiction, abuse, and gambling can destroy many relationships and happiness. Habits can destroy your financial resources, which could affect your job and the ability to pay for your home, automobile, or other bills. Bad habits can cause health problems and death; therefore, if you need to change, it must happen quickly. Don't let your personal habits rob you of a prosperous future. Everyone with a serious habit must go through a transformation phase and seek true deliverance. It takes a lot of hard work to overcome a long and serious habit, but the victory of change comes when you believe in yourself. There are things that can cause habits to be extended and slow down the process of change. Habits can be caused by experimenting, copying others, loneliness, rejection or loss, or constantly being disappointed; a personal failure can lead to the beginning of a habit. When struggling with a habit, you have to decide what is important. You have to make up your mind to begin the process. If your mind is not sure, then changing the situation is unlikely. Sometimes, you want to change because someone wants you to, but the decision begins within you to initiate the change of an old habit into a better situation.

Chapter 16
Focus on Change

I want to explore a topic that affects change. The topic of focus (focusing) is very vital when dealing with areas of change, whether they are mental, physical, or life changes. It takes consistency and focus to bring about positive outcomes when dealing with change. In most cases, you must be very detailed oriented with your plan in order to achieve the results you seek. Some people go into a situation with little thought given to the task, which leads to a negative result. The lack of consistency and focus can derail, hinder, and disrupt change. It takes a strong dose of courage and strength in order for change to happen. Focus is not always easy, but it's necessary. Lack of focus can be caused by being double-minded or torn on a certain issue. You have to zone in on what needs to happen and implement a plan that results in the desired outcome.

For change to be fully effective, you must be determined to go forward, no matter what obstacles appear. The enemy wants to bring about confusion and distractions when he sees that you are heading in a good direction. The devil doesn't want to see a change that will lead you closer to God. I've been through many tough situations in my life where focus was necessary in order to complete a task. Focus can get you through tough situations. The worse the situation, however, the tougher it can be to focus. Some situations can totally disrupt our thinking and feelings. I have learned at this stage of my life that God is the only one who can get me through some difficult situations. When dealing with serious life changes, the one thing that is under constant pressure is your mind (mental stability). Your mind has to be stable and mentally structured to handle serious life issues. There's very little preparation that can be done for death, natural disasters, sudden sickness, and so on, which can cause drastic changes to your life. It takes a solid mental foundation to get through the rigors of emotional storms. Emotional storms can be just as devastating as natural storms. An emotional storm can be as destructive to the mind as a tornado, wiping out every thought of hope, joy, peace, and positive foundations that you have in your mind-set. A tornado will destroy everything in its path, and an emotional tornado will attack every mental thing in its path. Emotional storms can be so destructive they leave a path of despair, hurt, loss, and devastation. Change is most difficult when caused by a life-altering circumstance. Just like any natural storm, there has to be a place to take refuge from the storm. Refuge can be hard to find, but you must seek it. A refuge could be a friend, a place, or a state of mind. In my storms, I find that talking to God and getting in his presence brings me tranquility.

One thing that's guaranteed is that a storm doesn't last forever. When things are really dark and gloomy around you, it can be hard to maintain focus. When you have positive people in your life, they can be a bridge to your peace of mind and happiness. Everyone needs a friend or loved one to talk to and receive good, sound advice from. When dealing with the difficulties of change, a stable environment is very beneficial. A house is secure when the structure is strong. When the foundation of a house is stable, it's secure. You just have to look to God to restore your peace of mind and give you direction on how to go on. Trials and tribulations will occur in your life and cause some type of change. I find peace from my problems when I get into the Word of God and remember the tough situations he brought me through. There were times when I didn't always trust God, and some situations still test my faith. For most people, their faith is seen by how they deal with problems or changes. Most of the time, their faith is forgotten, depending on the severity of the situation. Many people won't doubt their beliefs and faith when the situation isn't that serious, but when it's a life-changer, then faith is often in question. I've been through some rough changes in my life, but God always provides a way out.

When dealing with tragedy, job loss, or personal trials, faith is tough to maintain when you can't see that the situation has brought about a great void in your life. Once you lose your faith, you can lose your purpose. Once you lose your purpose, you can lose your focus. After you lose your focus, then you can lose your position.

Being well-positioned mentally is more important than being set up physically. Your life experiences will challenge your stability, mentally and physically. Change requires a mental infrastructure to be in place in order to initiate change, endure it, maintain it, and show progress when dealing with it. I can truly say that even at the age of thirty-six, I'm still learning to totally put my trust is God to make it through tough changes. One of the most difficult changes I've endured in my life was when I lost my father. My father was everything to me for such a long time, and going on with life without him has been hard.

Before my dad died, there was a change that really affected my entire family. After thirty-four years of marriage, my mom and dad decided to get a divorce. You might think that having children between the ages of thirty-two and thirty-six, they'd be able to deal with it, but that is furthest from the truth. My family has always been tight and close. Therefore, the news of our parents divorcing was truly surreal. We were all brought up to be about family. This was a devastating change to deal with, mainly because the environment had been consistent for thirty-three years. We could always count on going to the family home and seeing my mom and dad, but this was all about to change.

When my parents split up, there was a lot of he said/she said. When the talk of divorce manifested, there became bitter moments, and secrets began to surface. We were so devastated; it tore up my entire family. You don't always think a situation is supposed to change, but you can be sure that change will eventually come to everyone. When it was evident that my parents' marriage couldn't be repaired, change came knocking. Things came out that caused all of my siblings to truly resent my dad, but the biggest resentment was the fact that our family was changing. Divorce is an example of one thing in life that signifies change. Divorce is known to happen, but it's something you can prepare for. My life had always involved having Mom and Dad around; it was very hard to go through this metamorphosis called divorce. I wasn't ignorant to the chance that it could happen, but some things in life, you just don't expect. I had experienced my share of change. Although I was an adult, the divorce was a tough situation to go through.

My first initial reaction was that it happens to many families, but things wouldn't change that much. I never knew that things would take a turn that almost destroyed all the relationships within the family. During this process, many secrets were uncovered, which led to my parents' divorce. There were many times I lost faith in the concept of family. Up until this point, I thought that there was still hope for our family because my parents had been together for so long. In today's society, marriages often don't last long. The divorce rate is relatively high, and it's getting worse. I was able to hold to the fact that my parents had lasted thirty-three years, but I didn't know that the clock would soon stop. I go from being able to see my dad every day to seeing him a couple times a month. I went from talking to him every day to only once or twice a week.

There were so many norms that changed once they divorced. At first, because of the hard feelings that I harbored, I wouldn't talk to him at all. I couldn't believe that my dad, whom I admired greatly, would compromise his teachings on marriage. Once they made the decision to go their separate ways, Dad moved about two hours away. I know that many people in life probably have parents living in other states or countries that they don't get to talk to or see, but I never thought this type of change would happen to me. Oftentimes in life, you take people, jobs, families, and lifestyles for granted. This situation caused a great altering because of the relationship that my siblings and I shared with our dad. I can say that it takes a strong circle of loved ones to get you through when tough times and changes occur.

Over the next few years, my life continued to change; my dad was not only my mentor, he was my spiritual leader. During the time of my parents' separation, another change took place: Dad retired and turned his pastoral position over to me. I was now being called on to take over his ministry during all of these personal issues. Change doesn't do well with timing, but it makes you begin to tell time. When change presents itself, you can't help but look at the timing of the situation. The strain with my dad and my siblings continued for the next four years. The one thing that hurt the most was that I was extremely close to my dad, which caused me to have an emotional breakdown. Our communication became little to none; I wanted more but didn't know how to re-establish it. One day, as I prayed, the Holy Spirit told me that I couldn't go forward in my spiritual walk until I forgave him. God also instructed me to help my siblings with their anger and hatred. It took a few years, but my family finally started forgiving our dad, and we reconnected. A great moment in my life that helped seal the forgiveness was when my dad was able to attend my wedding. I struggled for a long time, contemplating not inviting him, but God would not have been pleased with me, and it would have hurt my dad. I had to realize that it was time to let it go and move forward. I knew that things happened in life, but change was necessary.

My siblings and I eventually restored our relationship with our dad, and the timing couldn't have been better. Then, a short time later, he got sick and passed away, but we can say that we made things all right with him before he died. That is why you have to live, love, forgive, and move forward because none of us know how much time we have. Tomorrow is not promised to anyone; therefore, you should do the very best to get the most out of life and enjoy every moment you can. You must have a direction of where you want to go. You must also be able to listen when you're given instructions.

Sometimes, you may be able to help others who are dealing with things you already went through. Therefore, throughout your life, you come into contact with many people who need direction. The only true way of knowing if you're on the right track is by deciding what track you must be on. What you're willing to walk away from something that has no benefit to your life, God will bring the right thing to you. You have to be willing to walk away from some old stuff, which continues to hinder your new stuff. Your change may cause people to walk away from you, but you have to see that as an opportunity for you. At one time in my life, I thought something was wrong with me because I was alone, but I had no clue that I was being positioned for a stellar life; everyone can't go with you when you are progressing. I had to see that God was promoting me, and when you are being promoted, that means you've outgrown a situation. I had to outgrow some people and places. My mind had to be renewed in order for me to go further in my life.

I look back and see how all of my challenges have made me into a God-fearing, believing, and strong-willed servant. When you constantly have people around you who you lean on, it makes you comfortable and can weaken you in the area of self-confidence. You should never get too complacent because you'll lose that attention and focus. When getting complacent, you miss details and surprises you should be watching for. There are times I got too comfortable, and it ended up costing me time, money, strength, and health. You're going to need that focus put solely on God. I had to learn to lean on him as well as realize that as long as someone else was there in his place, I would never give him the focus he deserved. The definition of *complacent* is to be unconcerned and satisfied with things while not wanting to change them. You tend to stop looking at things because you want them to stay the same, which causes you to be unconcerned. At the moment you become unconcerned, the enemy gained control. At this point, you're not even expecting anything to happen, but this is when you get tricked and are open to an attack from the devil.

Chapter 17

Five Senses for Change
(See, Smell, Taste, Touch, Hear)

Seeing Change

Let's look at the five senses and how they play a part in change. Seeing is one of the five senses. When you think about it, this is probably the most important of the senses, but it's also the one sense that gets fooled the most. You tend to see what you want to see. Seeing is a physical sense as well as an emotional sense. Your mind can create a picture that you physically don't see in front of you. Your physical sense of seeing can form a picture that your mind can't see at all. When I think about the sense of *see,* I think about the word *vision.* There are a couple of ways to look at this word. It could denote a picture that I can view in my mind or an image of something to come. Also, I could just view it as the ability to have sight. In either aspect, it should benefit me when I know that this sense can be the reason I believe that change can be something great for me and my life. In order to envision change, you have to see change. Seeing change must happen emotionally, mentally, and physically. You have to envision change in order to achieve success. Another aspect of the word *seeing* is that it means to be aware. Awareness is important to change due to the fact that you have to be mindful and knowledgeable of the task at hand. When you are aware, you are focused and paying attention.

Seeing has to be an attribute of faith. The Bible says, "Now faith is the substance of things hoped for and the evidence of things not seen" (KJV).

The phrase "not seen" in that scripture is a visual statement, stating that faith can play a big part with the sense of *seeing*. Faith is simply believing as well as knowing, but not actually physically seeing. In regard to faith, you need to see it through your spiritual eyes. When you are dealing with change, your mental or physical sight will determine the success of changing a situation. When you are faced with decisions without the right mind-set and vision, you can sometimes miss out on what God wants you to see. As a matter of fact, if you give up before accomplishing the necessary changes in areas of obtaining your peace, hope, and happiness, then you get what you see. A clear mind helps you to see things more clearly; it allows you to process things with a rational approach. People often need to have someone give specific accounts of what they're looking for in order to believe. If you believe, then you should be able to walk by faith and not by sight. When you can have faith and believe, then your faith can be your eyes. Instead of seeing it for yourself, trust in what God says to you.

I remember reading years ago in the Bible about a prophet who heard what others couldn't see. The prophet saw what others couldn't hear. The prophet Elijah told King Ahab that the rain was going to cease, and until God spoke, it would not rain again until he heard the release from God. King Ahab could not see the signs and just believed in what he saw and not the words of Elijah. The ability to see was vital, but are you seeing things mentally, spiritually, and physically? The rain stopped as the prophet said and only returned when God spoke. In 1 Kings 18, Elijah told King Ahab that he heard the sound of the abundance of rain. Remember: Your faith can serve as your seeing. When your faith is your sight, then God is pleased. People tend to see what they want to see when things are not good or when something suits them. In order to walk, you have to see where you are going.

Elijah didn't see the rain in the natural sense, but he saw it in a vision. He went up to the top of the mountain and got down on his knees to pray. He told his servant to go up to the mountain and look out toward the sea, but the servant came back and said that he didn't see anything. Elijah instructed him to go back up and look out a total of seven times. It was only until the seventh time that the servant saw a miracle forming before his eyes, as he looked out toward the sea. The servant finally did see something he wasn't expecting. As long as he had no expectations, he saw nothing. The moment he looked with conviction, he saw a sign from God, in which he saw a cloud coming up out of the sea in the image of a man's hand. I think if he had approached the instructions with more passion and desire, he would have seen the hand a lot sooner. You may think if you don't see it, you won't believe it. You have to approach things with an open mind. Change requires you to have an open mind.

To sum up the story of Elijah and the servant, when the servant saw the cloud in the form of a hand, he realized that what he was seeing was evidence of the Lord God responding to Elijah; he knew that something was about to happen. The servant knew this was not a normal occurrence. Elijah wanted the servant to bear witness that God was about to send rain into the desert. Therefore, you have to see change, but you have to trust God and have faith.

Chapter 18
Smelling Change

Another one of our senses is the ability to smell. With some changes, you have to smell change, which means that you have to sense it coming. You can be miles away from a place and still smell the aroma of something in the air, which is primarily the result of something with a strong natural fragrance as well as something that may be cooking. You can walk into an area and noticed a substance is giving off an aroma or illuminating smell. You may not see it, but you smell it. Change can be anticipated this way. In order to smell change, you will have to rely on your instincts. The dictionary meaning of *smell* is "to detect." This is an interesting aspect of change. It's why you have to be focused because your instincts will be a strong factor in detecting that change is needed. When I think of smell, I think about something drawing me to a place mentally or physically. When you smell change, the very thing that draws you into an area will need attention. Smelling change means something you've picked up is coming your way. Smelling change can mean that something's out there that you should be going after. Earlier, I said that sometimes, you have to initiate change. You have to smell it and pursue it. I've heard athlctes say they could smell victory. I believe the statement was driven off their confidence.

You can smell change when the culture around you seems to draw you a certain way. I will say that not all smells are good smells, which is why you have to be sharp and stay on top of things to ensure that you make the right choice. You have to make sure your smell is pinpoint and on the money. The nose knows, but are you trusting of your nose? Some aromas will always get your attention. Look over your own life and see what things have gotten your attention. You will find that as you were drawn to whatever it was, you had the choice to come from behind it. Then, the next step for you was to use your instincts. I'm not saying that every situation of change can be detected, but you have to be aware of the signs when they are there to be recognized. The last thing I'll say about smelling change is that you cannot ignore it or deny it. If you are sensing something on the horizon, why not examine what is manifesting and get a good jump on it? Don't wait too late to put some things in motion after you know for yourself what you've detected.

Chapter 19

Tasting Change

Taste is something we are all good at. We're all familiar with what it means to taste something. When you taste something, you're trying it out to see whether it's something you can acquire a taste for or dismiss it as something that's not good to you. When you taste something, you then have the opportunity to accept it or reject it. Usually, tasting something tells you whether it's pleasing to your taste buds or you're not thrilled by what you just tasted. To taste something is the same as trying something. It takes you to keep trying it in order to develop a taste for something. When you have a taste for something, you're not really satisfied until you get it. Life can be this way, as well. You want to know that if something you're about to do or a step you're about to make is the right thing for you. In life, you have to try many different things in order to find what works.

I'm intrigued by the definition of *taste*. Typically, when people think about taste or tasting, they think in regards to food or drink. The definition of *taste* that caught my attention is that it also means "to get experience or take a liking to something." I like the idea of getting experience. When you think about making some changes, it may take you stepping outside the box and trying some different ideas in order to find the right one for you. Even if things don't work out, then at least it gave you experience, which you now know that you've tried it before. When difficult moments are all that you see, you have to try a different method in order to win over that situation. After you've gone so long without some good things happening for you, you have to taste something new in order to add to what you like. I used to go places wanting to do the same thing all the time, but this keeps you from expanding your experiences; you never know if something would have been better only because you were not willing to try something new. Just like victory, you have to taste it. Victory should be appealing enough that you want to taste it. I like to go to new places to try new things. People miss out on so much because they're not willing to try some new and different things. When you can taste change, it's because you're tired of the same results and ready for something else. You have to want things to be better in your life. In order to do that, you have to try some new things and draw your own conclusion about it. When you accumulate victories and other good moments in your life, you'll definitely want more. The one thing for you to remember is that when you can taste change, you will have to put yourself in a position to satisfy that hunger. The urge to succeed should be the taste that motivates you to change.

Touching Change

What could I mean by touching change? Looking back at things in general, this thought of touching change reminds me of some earlier points in the book. Touching change is when you've gotten to a certain point in your life but lose that place. You work so hard to make it, but then you allow a situation to cause you to lose that experience. Touching change could also suggest there was something that you put your finger on but let it slip away. You came into contact with the necessary means and resources to make a change, but you didn't sustain it. Most people say, "I came so close." If you know that you were once that close or you're that close right now, don't give up, but keep grinding in order to accomplish that which you set out to accomplish. You can't let someone's opinion derail your hopes and dreams. Most people will not see it like you see it, but you have to keep working in order for it to be fulfilled. Touching change is something we all experience, which means that we are right there, but fear, rejection, and other emotions may cause us to take our hands off. *Touch* also means that you have to feel it. You have to feel what you want to happen. You have to feel what you need to happen. Feeling it is driven by your will and passion. When you're motivated, you'll feel an overwhelming desire to make whatever changes you need in every part of your life to have that success for your future.

The one thing that I pray for is that people have peace and joy in their lives. You face so many obstacles throughout your life; this is something everyone should possess. I believe even rich people struggle in some areas of their lives. Money doesn't make a home. Money can't buy you health. Money can't make people love you. Therefore, what is it that you got in you that will be special to someone else? You just have to feel what's needed in order to visualize the steps to achieve what you're striving to achieve. Once you've got your finger on it, which means you figured it out, the rest is up to you to get it done.

Hearing Change

The last of the senses to associate with change is hearing. Hearing is something that requires details. Hearing requires listening. That statement right there is a mouthful. The question is, who are you going to listen to? In order to hear change, you have to perceive that what you're hearing is accurate and clear. You never want to move so fast that you end up right back where you started. When you talk about the word *hearing*, you have to pay attention. You're the perfect person to assess your life and what is good and bad about it. When hearing change, you have to pay close attention to the particular areas that you want to change, but also be aware of the environment. You have to perceive when the time is right to move. Maybe staying where you are is better for the moment, but you have to hear from your surroundings. It would be nice if everyone had someone they could bounce thoughts off of, but not everyone has a mentor in their lives.

Your hearing informs you. You just have to make sure that things around you are not too loud. You can't hear clearly if things are loud around you. I can most assuredly say that when you have a peaceful atmosphere, you can hear clearly, and your thinking is intensified. We all want to get it right the first time, but most people have a hearing problem. Many times, they don't want to hear constructive criticism or even listen to advice coming from someone who has been there before. I have seen that when someone's emotions and feelings are involved, it's more difficult for them to want to hear anything. You have to always be open to change, but you should definitely hear when change is necessary.

I implore you to hear within yourself when something is not right or something is going left. Your life will be so much better once you can listen to the signs and hear the desire from within when change is now. Always know that you are not crazy; what you're hearing may be different from what others suggest, but analyze and pay attention, and you'll be able to discern if what you're hearing is spot-on. After you know what you know and hear what you hear, make the changes.

Chapter 20

Momentum

There are far more people who can do than people who choose not to do. Confidence can carry you a long way. I know specifically that there are four things God can't do, which are lie, fail, change, and nothing. Of course, it's your decision whether you want to believe in God or not, but I have history on my side: He has never failed me, as I have oftentimes failed myself. Still, I overcame my failings, and now I am enjoying life to the fullest every day at this particular stage of my life. God can't lie, and he will not lie. When I read the Bible and see it talking about my life, then I know he doesn't lie. So many times, I've seen God come through for me, even when I didn't believe in him or myself. This is proof again that God will not fail me. I thank God that he never changes on me, although I have changed on him so many times. He never stopped loving me, with some forgiveness added in there, as well. As I stated earlier in this book, there is nothing that's too hard for God; therefore, there's nothing that he can't do. You'll just have to get that. The fact that God loves you and me should tell you that he will not just sit on the throne, looking down on his people, and stand idly by, without doing anything for us. There are so many things that God has done for us even when we didn't deserve it.

Since we know that he loves us dearly, now is the time to build on that momentum. Some things you can do can provide you with momentum. *Momentum* means to move with force and speed. You have the strength in you, and you should not let anyone tell you differently. You have it in you to succeed. When you experience a string of positive moments and outcomes in your life, the momentum builds up. Right then, you have to become so focused and motivated to continue the good vibes. I understand that not everything will go your way in life, but when you experience some great and awesome goodness beginning to happen for you, live in that moment and build on it. Your emotional peace can propel you to do great things. Some people get to a place where some amazing things begin to happen, but they stop the intensity and hard work needed to keep it coming. That momentum will carry you all the way to your desired ending.

Momentum builds up your confidence and sharpens your focus. This book was inspired to build up your hope and momentum; you worked too hard to give up now. You are powerful when you know and recognize that power within you. When you get that momentum going, you'll feel unstoppable. When you are rolling along with that momentum, you'll feel invincible. Once you get that feeling, sustain it and maintain it. Don't let anything cause you to have a letdown. You keep pressing through the dark moments because the one thing that must come is daylight. Things can only be dark for a short period because light is inevitable. I have never seen a storm that did not pass. You develop maturity from certain things you learn choices you made. It feels good to have that energy, to feel that you can do almost anything and accomplish greater things when you put your mind to it. You can overcome so much with maturity, patience, and drive. Even though some things are not where they need to be, it can't last a lifetime. Problems and pain are going to come, but help and victory must come as well. I realize in this life that sometimes, you are your worst critic and your worst enemy. Don't be a pessimist about change, but become an optimist for change. Embrace the growth that you are about to experience. Joy and peace should be a daily goal, no matter what situation you face. We all will have our ups and downs, but I have made it my mission to have way more ups than downs. I choose to ride that wave of momentum until the day I leave this earth.

After you accomplish what you set out for, you should want more for your life and help others get to that place of prosperity. Isaiah 52 says in verse 1 to "put on your strength" (KJV). This just opens up my motivation to a much higher level. You should always know that you have to find the strength within yourself. There are times when you may not have someone there to pick you up, but you have strength and power inside you. Sometimes, you're so used to people being your life support that you forget to support yourself. It's great to have people in your corner, but how do you function when they are not available? God is there, and so are you.

Defeat comes easily when you think you can't win. Who goes into a battle expecting to lose? Just because you've lost a battle or two doesn't mean you are destined to lose every time. We've all had our moments, but you have to take a situation and make it your own by looking at the positives and building upon that so that the outcomes will change. You should never want to go through life with a defeated mind-set. I've learned to utilize when something good happens or when I get a positive result; I use it to my advantage to build up the momentum to have even greater moments. Momentum requires some specific choices that must be made in order to keep the momentum flowing. I've been talking about this word: *better*. Your momentum should push you to better. You should want better. You should experience better. You should think better, and then I assure you that you will see better. Sometimes, it's difficult to see anything other than problems, but you have to want better, which will help your motivation to make it happen.

As I was writing this chapter on momentum, I noticed that the word had a keyword within the word to make the word define itself. *Momentum* has a root word of *moment*. You have to make the most out of the moment. It is in the moment that you can find your opening, door, or assurance of outcome. It is up to you to maximize the moment. Your mind is sharpest when faced with hard times because it will push you to go beyond normal thinking into a deeper and detailed mentality. You have to maximize the moment to create positive change and culture in your life. The moment something tough hits you is when strength must follow. That very moment you feel like giving up, remember the journey and the process that got you to a better place; that is the same moment that you should reconsider quitting and begin equipping yourself for the fight. Every moment carries a reaction, but the constant has to be your effort to overcome.

Maximize means to get the greatest use out of something. Your momentum is important to you just because it builds up such a high degree of confidence as well as awareness. What I mean by awareness is that you get a clear view of what is reality, and then you can determine how you want things to go without always having the situation dictate it. Whenever you find yourself picking up steam, it gives you a sense of invincibility. You then feel that power and strength, which makes you feel that you can do it. I often tell myself, *Yes, I can.* This is because of momentum that I've been able to experience. The more you take advantage of the moment, the more you see the momentum opportunity. You then start the process of building up the momentum that you need.

At some point in all of our lives, we need a string of good things to happen. I've never been a person who believes in luck. I just don't believe in it. I hear of a person having good luck or bad luck, but I just believe that certain circumstances can be attributed to their choices or decisions. There are definitely some things that you can't figure out, but you still have a mind that can produce the choice to change. *Luck* means something happening by chance that could be either good fortune or bad fortune. See, this really doesn't add up just because that's how life is, but just because something bad happened doesn't mean that it has to continue. Bad or good luck to me is associated with a string of events, either good or bad. Right there, that tells me that you can either determine the string of events or put some things in place to change the occurrence of things happening. Whether you believe in luck, good or bad, just know that at times, you play a part in outcomes and solutions.

I am the solution and not the question. I must say that there is no greater feeling in the world than having confidence and feeling that you can conquer the world. I'm not naïve to think that life is not difficult, but you have to ensure that you are doing everything possible to be great while hoping for a greater outcome. I have learned to take control of my actions and words, which gives me a better chance of having a controlled outcome. Honestly, you may fail and come short of aspirations whether you worked so hard, but things just didn't work out for you, but you have to work for you. You will not always be successful in everything, but one good success can push you into many successes.

My encouragement to you is that you never look down on yourself and never doubt your abilities. Things come and go as well as people. I can cry or I can construct. I can construct a better path for me and mine. The impact that you can make to a situation can be just what you need to get through the tough moments. Learn to be a consistent person who smiles and does things to make yourself happy. Sometimes, you can put so much time in other people while all the time forgetting about yourself. I understand that there are certain people and things that require your attention, but just don't forget about you. If you are down, you can't be effective. If you are sick, you can't be effective. If you are in a bad position, how can you help others?

My point to you is that you matter. Take advantage of the good that you see and take advantage of the good moments that you experience so that you can build up a strong foundation for success. Everything in your life should be sound, which suggests that everything should be at a peace in your life. Mind, body, and spirit should all be sound. You have to consistently keep a thought in mind of *Never again*. You may have dealt with some challenging moments and issues that you never want to go back to; stay motivated and live out that thought of *Never again*. Never again should you allow the harm to overtake your heart. Never again allow negative people to cause you to be down, but build yourself up into knowing that you are somebody and there is an inner strength in you, but that inner strength must have inner peace. Once you get peace in your life, guard it and never let it go. It feels good to have peace because when you have peace, joy will follow.

Stay encouraged, stay strong, stay uplifted.

You were born to win, and you have been given a charge to change. In whatever you do, stay with the Lord Jesus Christ. Jesus is the way, the truth, and the life.

I want to end this book with a prayer:

In the name of Jesus, first of all, I just want to thank you for everything that you do and continue to do in our lives. I thank you for life today. I just want to honor you, God, for keeping us through every trial, challenge, and obstacle that we faced. Thank you for loving us even when we were not obedient to your will. I pray that you grant peace on everyone; let them experience the joys of life. I pray strength so everyone will continue to strive for greater things and to be better in every facet of their lives. Lord, I believe that you died so that we would have a greater, more abundant life. Now, Lord, bless those who continue to struggle with the cares of this life and give them the power to overcome every stage of change that they have to endure. I just want to thank you in advance of the blessings that are to come to every reader, their homes, their families, and everyone connected to them. Cover each and every one with the blood of Jesus, in the name of the Father, the son, Jesus Christ, and the Holy Spirit.

Amen.

Printed in the United States
By Bookmasters